MONKEY ON MY BACK!

MONKEY ON MY BACK!

Personal Reflections on Doing a PhD

Thomas J. Carroll

Copyright © 2014 by Thomas J. Carroll, PhD
All Rights Reserved

Published and printed in the United States of America

ISBN-13: 978-1502391476
ISBN-10: 1502391473

All Rights Reserved. This publication may not be reproduced, stored in a retrieval system, or transmitted in whole or in part, in any form or by any means, electronic, mechanical, photocopying, recording, or otherwise—with the exception of a reviewer who may quote brief passages in a review to be printed in a newspaper or magazine—without prior written permission from the author. Contact the author: tcarroll@apiconsult.com

Disclaimer:
This book is designed to provide general information on the subject matter covered. Rules and regulations, practices and the interpretation of the same regarding PhDs vary from one country and institution to another. Because each situation is different, the reader is advised to consult with his or her own adviser/local institution regarding that individual's specific situation.
Neither the author nor the publisher assume any responsibility for any errors or omissions, nor do they represent or warrant that the information, ideas, plans, actions on the subject matter covered herein is in all cases true, accurate or appropriate.

Book cover and interior design by Jean Boles
http://jeanboles.elance.com

DEDICATION

To Jane, Mick, Kieran and James

ACKNOWLEDGEMENTS

I would like to thank all who have contributed to the writing of this book, both directly and indirectly.

To my family—my wife, Jane, and sons, Mick, Kieran and James, I say thanks for putting up with my doing a PhD, my absences, long hours of writing and all the financial deprivations a PhD entails.

To my cousin, Jim—thanks for all your companionship through the final years of the PhD and while writing this book.

Thanks also to Jean Boles for the design of this book and book cover.

"All life is an experiment. The more experiments you make the better."

-Ralph Waldo Emerson

CONTENTS

Foreword 15
Chapter One: Introduction 23
    What is this book about? 23
    Who is this book for? 25
    What is a PhD? 26
    What you can expect from this book 28
    Process of Writing this Book 30
    Overview of the book 31
    Chapter One summary 32
Chapter Two: What it takes to get a PhD 33
    Costs involved in earning a PhD 33
        Financial cost 34
        Time cost with Family and Friends 35
        Earnings forgone 36
        Other opportunity costs 38
    Intelligence and the PhD 38
    Grit 42
    Hard work 44
    Motivation and getting a PhD 45
        Good reasons to do a PhD 49
    Personality and getting a PhD 51
    Skills and knowledge 52
    The support of others 53
    Chapter Two summary 53

Chapter Three: Getting Started With Your PhD 55
   Choosing a PhD programme 55
      Varieties of PhD programmes 56
      University rankings 59
   Financing your PhD 60
   Choosing your subject 61
      Long term personal planning 63
   Choosing a good Supervisor 65
      Qualities of a good Supervisor 67
      My experience 68
      How to find a good supervisor 72
      Try to understand your supervisor 73
      Parallels with business 74
   Chapter Three summary 75

Chapter Four: How to Make Progress 77
   Begin with the finish in mind 77
      Beware of the planning fallacy 79
   Visualisation 80
      Reinforcing your PhD vision 83
   Watch out for the rabbit trails 85
   Quit or never quit? 86
      The effects of doctoral attrition 89
   Focus on the NOW 93
   The PhD is an Iterative Process 95
   PhD by Kaizen 95
   Work with your supervisor 96

Time management 97
    The power of habit 98
    Chunk down your work 101
    Chunk down your time 103
Dealing with procrastination 104
Don't be alone 106
There are no straight lines 107
    Chronology of my PhD 108
Working and doing a PhD 111
How to manage stress 113
Chapter Four summary 116

Chapter Five: Completing the PhD, Graduation & Beyond 119

The End Game 119
    The Viva Voce 121
So you got your PhD— What Next? 123
Careers for PhD holders 125
    Reflections on my Post PhD Career 127
    Earning potential of people with PhDs 130
    Expectations on completing the PhD 133
    Imposter Syndrome 134
    Sunk Costs in Careers 135
Higher education is changing 137
    Is the PhD still relevant? 138
Chapter Five summary 139

Chapter Six: Conclusion 143

- What I learned from the PhD process 144
  - You are the boss 144
  - Develop grit—learn to persist 145
  - Manage your time well and finish fast 145
  - Plan well 146
  - Tiny changes mean huge results 146
  - Work hard 147
  - Develop good habits 147
  - Manage stress 148
  - You are intelligent enough 149
  - Begin again each day 150
  - Think about life after the PhD 150
  - You need a good team 152
  - Some good luck also helps 153
- How I have benefited by doing a PhD 153
  - I have earned an impressive credential 156
  - I have developed my Grit 157
  - I have set and achieved a big Goal 157
  - Being more self-reflective 158
  - Better at critical thinking 159
  - I have learned valuable skills and specialist knowledge 160
  - Satisfaction at making a contribution 162
- The downside of doing a PhD 162
  - There is a high opportunity cost to getting a PhD 163
  - Will anyone care about my research? 163
- Next steps 164

About the Author 165
  Contact the Author/Leave Feedback 166
References and Useful Resources 167
  Useful PhD related Books and Articles 167
  PhD/Education Related Online Resources 174
  Other Useful Books and Articles 177
  Useful Online Resources... 179
  Useful computer software...181

FOREWORD

Nearly a year ago now as I write this—July 2012—I was preparing for my Viva Voce (oral) exam and nearing the end of my PhD. For six years I had struggled to make progress and to complete and submit my thesis. By the end of 2012, I had successfully graduated with my PhD degree. In writing this book I wanted to get all my thoughts and reflections written down before the memory faded and I forgot all the pain I went through to get this degree! I have no doubt that time dulls the memories. In hindsight, everything can sometimes look easier than it was. It's a nice vantage point to look back, having completed the degree and already know the outcome. I started my PhD way back in 2006, and it took me six years to complete; in the meantime, I had grown older, balder, greyer, and my children had caught up to me in height! A lot can happen in six years. Of course you can do a PhD much quicker, and in this book I will show you how to avoid the mistakes I made which prolonged my PhD woes.

This is the book I wish that I had read and acted upon before embarking on my own PhD! It is highly likely if I had known what I know now and what was ahead of me, I would never have done a PhD at all and pursued other goals instead. In many ways I did not realise what I was getting myself into when I started out on my PhD. This book will help you to realise just how tough getting a PhD is so that if you do decide to set out on this journey you will be prepared. There is no point in setting out for a polar expedition in shorts and tee shirt—you won't get far! And as you will need special equipment for a polar expedition, I believe this book will better equip you to prepare for your PhD expedition.

In my own particular case, I began my PhD at age 39. I had a wife and three children to support, so I was working full time while doing my PhD. And just to make it even more challenging, I also survived a civil conflict in Kenya, moved countries and continents and changed careers as well. Apart from the obvious obstacles, I also struggled against my own negative thoughts and lack of confidence in my ability to complete the PhD. My negative thinking slowed me down and made the PhD experience more difficult and longer to complete than it should have. The risk is that the longer you spend doing a PhD the more that can happen to distract you. People are born and others may die. Children grow into young women and men. In the meantime you have to live with the PhD like an unwanted companion. I have heard it described as a monkey on your back (hence the title of this book). You will not be able to fully enjoy your holidays, time off, weekends etc. for the duration of the PhD. *You will have the monkey on your back,* and you will feel guilty when relaxing! The monkey is a constant, nagging feeling—no matter what else you are doing, the PhD is there with you. It is a dark cloud hanging over you from which you cannot escape.

Some people are born to academic work. I am not one of those, and I struggled throughout the process. I'm not a high flyer for whom the PhD was a breeze. I'm not the best student—certainly not the brightest, the most organised etc. I am just an average student. For me doing a PhD was very difficult; I see myself as a somewhat marginal PhD candidate who struggled through the process. I think my experience of doing a PhD is valuable as someone who courted failure. If you avoid the mistakes I made, you will certainly get through the PhD process much faster and with less pain. If I can get a PhD, then you can, too. I struggled and I failed; I learned from failure and then I overcame failure, and in the end, I turned failure into success. As a result of my own struggles and failure I feel that I have much to share. What I am saying in this book is that this is what I did, this was my journey, these were the obstacles I came upon and this is what I had to do to cross the finish line and successfully complete my PhD. If this book teaches you at least one thing to make your own PhD journey a little bit easier, or even makes you think more deeply before starting a PhD and helps you decide if a PhD is for you or not, then I will have achieved my goal in writing this book. It will certainly have been worth your while to take the time to read the book.

A recurring question which I asked myself during my PhD years was why did I put myself through this pain? Why did I start this PhD? Writing this book has been like a mental cleansing exercise for me and it also has allowed me to analyse why I started my PhD, what I did, what I learned about the process and why I succeeded in the end. This book is partly my own attempt to process and understand what I have done with the six years of my life spent working on my PhD.

Before embarking on the PhD I had completed two masters and a bachelor's degree; however, nothing I had done before had prepared me for the PhD. My PhD was totally self-directed research. My progress on my earlier degrees was dictated by coursework and exams—relatively easy. You are carried along by the group and the course schedule. For both master's degrees I was part of a class, and we individually carried out a minor thesis after the main part of the taught course. These theses were of three months duration but were not necessarily a good preparation for doing a PhD. The PhD was a different kettle of fish altogether—much longer and tougher in every way. With a PhD, if it's to be, it's up to you—you are largely on your own, and that is hard, really hard.

Through sharing my story I want to help you to be more aware of the challenges and opportunities and help you to think through your own reasoning for doing a PhD. Through this book I want to challenge you to think! You need to reflect carefully before starting a PhD; this is a lengthy, difficult and costly project. The right time to quit a PhD is never to start, and this book will help you make a more informed decision before you even begin.

I believe that what I have to share can help others who may be doing or considering doing a PhD. The fact that I have endured the PhD process and eventually succeeded qualifies me to write this book. I am also qualified to write this book because I struggled and failed so much along the way. The experience of failure is important—I was successful in the end but I spent most of the process failing! I succeeded because I was doing things wrong, I learned the hard way, and then I started to do things right. I came to the point of nearly giving up my PhD, and I will share what brought me to that point and what I did to rectify the situation. However, even if I had failed to complete the PhD, I would still have had very valuable information to share!

> *"It's too bad failures don't give seminars. Wouldn't that be valuable?"*
>
> - Jim Rohn, Entrepreneur

In this book I present what worked for me, and I hope that you can find some things here to help you. I want you, the reader, to learn from my experiences. Through these pages I want to share my mistakes and failures and explore what I did to eventually succeed.

> *"Learn from the mistakes of others. You can't live long enough to make them all yourself."*
>
> - Eleanor Roosevelt, American First Lady

There are many books which deal with epistemology, research methods, statistics etc. This is not one of those books. This book looks at the big picture—what is a PhD? Why would you want one? And, how to survive and successful complete a PhD once you start the process. It also covers tools and issues related to motivation and time management. This book focusses a lot more on the psychology of getting a PhD rather than the mechanics of it. Sometimes we can get caught up in the academic details and never look at the big picture! As with everything you do, you need to begin with the end in mind! Why suffer through a PhD only to find out after a number of years of hard slog that it's not really what you wanted. Careful thought is required—you must look right to the end of the PhD and beyond.

When I started my PhD I was focused on the academic aspect of doing the PhD—theoretical frameworks, literature reviews, statistics etc. With all of this in mind, it's easy to forget the big picture issues. I want to remind you of these and other issues which may not be so obvious (or are so obvious we overlook them!) but are really important to your success. It's not just about being good in the laboratory or in statistics. Yes, these are important skills; however, these skills can be learned and we can obsess with these technical aspects of the PhD. But it's really important that we get our heads right as well.

The PhD is just a large personal project, and skills learned while doing a PhD can also be used to achieve other tough goals. This started out as a book about doing a PhD, but I realised later that doing a PhD cannot be looked at in isolation. Doing a PhD is intertwined with all aspects of your life—who you are and how you think and act. There is no separate compartment called "doing a PhD." It is part of you, your life, your hopes and dreams, your psychology, your very being. In many ways, therefore, the book expands beyond the narrow confines of looking at the PhD from just an academic perspective. What started off as a project to capture reflections on the PhD process grew from there with the PhD as the backdrop. The PhD project touches on everything in your life. That is why I discuss the issues to do with personal development and personal effectiveness throughout this book. In order to be successful with this PhD project you need to develop yourself as a person.

You are the project manager and you need to manage the PhD project well to be successful. Like any challenging project, you are going to learn a lot about yourself. You will likely go through rough patches where you will just feel like quitting. You will have to learn how to *manage yourself*.

This is not a book of answers to all your PhD questions. This book asks many questions which only you can answer. However, these questions are very valuable and can save you considerable misery if you spend the time and effort needed to answer them.

"The scientist is not a person who gives the right answers; he's one who asks the right questions."

- Claude Lévi-Strauss, French anthropologist

I went through my own PhD in isolation, and it is comforting now to understand that what I experienced was similar to the experience of other PhD students. By writing this book, I hope to give you a better understanding of the PhD process so that you will not be faced with the same issues that I encountered—or, if and when you are, you will have a better understanding of how to deal with them as a result of reading this book.

Chapter One

Introduction

*"THINKING is hard work.
That's why so few people do it."*

- Henry Ford, American Industrialist

What is this book about?

The purpose of this book is to make you think! One thing I have learned from my own life experiences is that as human beings we don't think enough. Instead, we prefer subconscious driven action. Conscious thinking is hard work! I should have done a lot more thinking before starting my own PhD! This book takes a long-term perspective on doing a PhD and explores the bigger picture issues relating to doing a PhD, based on the author's own experience. Key questions are:

- What is a PhD?
- Why bother doing one?
- What can you do with a PhD?
- How can you get through the PhD process as quickly and smoothly as possible?

The book is only to set out arguments and counterarguments on doing a PhD; the decision, of course, is for the reader. I only want to open your eyes to ensure you are aware of some of the arguments for and against. At the end of the day it is your life and you have to decide how best to live it. If you do decide to do a PhD, the book also deals with how to survive and complete the study—what to do and what mistakes to avoid. Doing a PhD is like doing any big project, and the book deals with strategies to get this project done. It also explores quitting the PhD if that is the best option for you. I have personally made a good number of the mistakes that were to be made, but somehow I managed to turn things around, get through the process, and get my PhD. I want to share that experience with you.

This book is not about research methods, statistics or any other of the important subject areas involved in PhD research. It is about the big picture stuff (The *Why*), and hopefully, it will help you to focus and reflect on key issues. It is also about time management and how to make progress on your PhD once you start, along with how to cultivate the right mental attitude for PhD success. Your PhD is not done in isolation from you, the person—how you think and the other aspects of your life. It intersects with who you are; therefore, if you want to understand the PhD you have to have a broader focus than just on academics. There are numerous books about PhD research, some of which I have personally used and recommend; they are listed in the annex at the end of this book.

It's too easy to get bogged down in the technical details of a PhD and fail to see the big picture. This book is about taking a step back and looking at that bigger picture. If a PhD is wrong for you then reading this book can potentially save you a lot of money and from wasting years of your life. You really need to think long and hard before embarking on the PhD journey.

This book is based very much on my own musings and reflections on the PhD process and is supported with appropriate references as needed throughout the text.

Who is this book for?

This book is specifically for anyone already doing or contemplating doing a PhD. If you are currently doing a PhD and need some inspiration from an average student like myself who managed to succeed and complete the process (Okay, it did take me six years of my life!), then this book will help you achieve your goal. If you are doing a PhD already then this book will help you to finish and finish faster.

This book is also useful for anyone studying for other academic goals, such as a master's or undergraduate degree or looking for general lessons in goal achievement. Getting a PhD is just like finishing any other major goal in life which requires persistence and hard work to make it happen, and the lessons here can be applied towards other non-academic goals, such as writing a book or developing a website or business.

The book is also for the long-suffering family members, relatives and friends of anyone doing a PhD and will help them to understand what it's all about. They are in the PhD process as well and need to understand as much as possible about what doing a PhD entails. Perhaps you will be in a better position to advise your PhD student after reading this book on how he/she can manage this process better.

This book is aimed at those anywhere in the world who are interested in PhD study, although I am writing from an Irish perspective because I studied with an Irish university. However, the lessons contained here can be universally applied.

What is a PhD?

It is interesting for me that this is the first time I am really carefully examining the definition of what a PhD is now that I am finished! When doing a PhD things do not go in straight lines, and in my experience it is common to keep jumping back to understand or complete earlier stages in the PhD process. As you can see, in this case I have already finished my PhD and I am now going back to really understand what it is—which should be the very first step in the process!

My own definition of a PhD is hard work for which you don't get paid! Officially, a PhD is an abbreviation for Doctor of Philosophy. The title, Doctor of Philosophy, originates from the Latin expression philosophiae (love of wisdom). The words *doctor* and *doctorate* come from the Latin word docere, meaning "to teach." Dating back to nineteenth-century Germany (Noble, 1994), the PhD has changed very little since its inception. A PhD describes the third tier in the traditional hierarchy of university education (bachelor's degree, master's degree and then PhD).

A doctorate is usually based on at least three years graduate study and a dissertation and is the highest degree awarded for graduate study. Matt Might, Assistant Professor at the University of Utah in the USA has good online visual diagrams of what a PhD is, which show how a PhD pushes the boundary of knowledge in a certain area of expertise. (Please see: http://matt.might.net/articles/phd-school-in-pictures/.)

To graduate with a PhD you have to make a contribution to knowledge in your particular field of study. One way to do this is to publish in a peer reviewed journal, which demonstrates that what you have to say is of value.

You should be aware that entry requirements and what a PhD entails varies from one country to the next, and depending on where you live in the world, you need to check with your local university to understand local requirements. A PhD is not a single, well-defined qualification, and what a PhD is, how long it takes, and how it is examined, varies from one country to another. Despite variations in what a PhD is, the same broad lessons contained in this book still apply, as fundamentally, a PhD is a challenging goal achieved over a number of years. According to Stock and Siegfried (2006), the median time-to-degree for economics PhDs in the USA was near 5.5 years in 2002. In Canada, only about half of all students who enter PhD programs actually complete (Elgar, 2003). In general, a PhD is a challenging goal carried out over a number of years, and a large proportion of those who start will not complete for a variety of reasons. In the bigger scheme of things not that many people have PhDs. Earning a PhD degree is something that very few people manage to do. It's estimated that only about 1% of the U.S. population has a PhD, so it certainly puts you in a small group of people when you achieve PhD level.

What you can expect from this book

This book is based on the writer's personal account and reflections on doing a PhD or Doctor of Philosophy degree. The book shares a personal PhD experience and is intended to be simple and to the point, highlighting key lessons. Every student's experience of doing a PhD will vary from one case to another—this is my own experience. However, key issues and broad lessons will have commonalities from one student to another. Where appropriate I have supported my experience with reference to books, articles and online resources in relation to the issues presented in this book.

Based on my experience there are a number of important questions which need to be reflected upon. Questions are very important and you need to make sure that you are comfortable with these questions and your own answers to these questions. Effort now to answer these questions will pay big dividends. If you do not plan well then you might find that years later you went down the wrong path. The answers to these questions will be unique to yourself and your own particular circumstances and nobody else can answer these questions for you. It's your life and nobody else can make these decisions for you—you will be the one to live with the consequences of your own decisions. As regards the timing of looking at the issues highlighted in this book, you can only start from where you are now. You may be just thinking about doing a PhD or have already completed one. No matter what stage you are at, it is still useful to reflect on issues and questions raised here. We can only move forward from where we are!

Much of this book focusses on big picture stuff and not technical aspects of the PhD. This book is about the WHY and not so much about the HOW. The Why must come first—if you have a clear purpose it will propel you to success. As long as you have the Why there is nothing you cannot undertake, and that applies to a PhD as well as to any other goal in your life. Getting a PhD is just like trying to achieve any other big goal. You need a big vision. This book aims to get you clear on the Why by asking the tough questions. If you have a clear Why then you will be able to find the How—e.g. how to write a good research proposal, methodological skills, how to analyse data, statistics, academic writing etc. The mechanics of how to do research is covered in many other books and is not the main focus here. I will point you in the direction of some useful additional books and other resources on the How.

A key focus of this book is about being in the right frame of mind to succeed and how to keep motivated over such a long period of study (six years in my own case!). The focus on Why is hugely important to your success, not just in achieving your PhD within a reasonably short timeframe but also in what you will do after getting your PhD.

If you are already doing a PhD perhaps this book will inspire you to continue to the end of the process or perhaps it might just inspire you to quit! This is my own story, the story of my journey and my reflections on the PhD process. The PhD journey described in the book is my own; however, the fundamental issues and questions will be the same for all. I hope you can learn from my experiences.

One thing to be aware of is that this book is looking backwards at what happened during my PhD, and events can look different knowing the ending as I do now (I succeeded). We can change and distort memories looking backwards—a retrospective distortion of events. This hindsight bias is the inclination to see events that have already occurred as being more predictable than they were at the time. One thing which is interesting is that most of the time during my PhD I spent thinking that I would never finish. Certainly the outcome was always uncertain and in doubt. Looking at my personal diary entries from that time I can see the confusion. Most of the time, I spent thinking of quitting and failure. Most of the time, I spent thinking that I am not suited to do a PhD anyway. It was not until near that end—perhaps in the last six months—that things became more certain. That means that I spent over 90% of the time during the PhD process in a state of uncertainty, thinking of quitting and failing and how hard this was and how unsuited I was to do a PhD. Keep this in mind as you read through the book.

Process of Writing this Book

This book was written over a period of nearly two years. It was started around the time of my Viva Voce Exam (an oral exam at the end of the PhD) and before my graduation and extended to a year and a half after graduation. The process of writing this book was slow, in small daily doses, with plenty of time for contemplation and self-examination. This slow process allowed me plenty of time to read, research and reflected on my PhD experience. Insights would come to me—especially as I commuted to work in the mornings. I would capture these insights on my smartphone and add them to the book later. I would also listen to audio books on personal effectiveness/business-related topics on my daily commute to work, and ideas from the audio books would resonate with my own PhD experience and get me exploring new insights on my PhD which I had not considered before. As a result, this book has benefited immensely from this slow reflective writing approach. The book has expanded, evolved and deepened as I have ruminated on the issues involved in doing my PhD over time—this is a great strength of this book. Writing this book is very personal and scary for me—it exposes my own fears and weaknesses. A PhD does not happen in isolation, it happens as part of your life; so I am not just writing about the PhD but how it intertwines with life in general, and my personal life is intertwined in this book. However, I feel that if I do not share my own vulnerability, fears and weaknesses then the book will be much less useful. In writing this book I necessarily have to feel exposed as the author. I am not writing about the mechanics of doing the PhD; I am exposing my innermost thoughts, feelings and insecurities, which is scary for me but more useful to you, the reader.

Overview of the book

The first chapter introduces the book in a general sense and who the book is for. Chapter Two looks at what it takes to get a PhD. Chapter Three examines important issues, such as how to choose your subject for study and your PhD supervisor. It also looks at goal setting and the benefits and costs of doing a PhD. Chapter Four looks at how to make progress on your PhD once you start and issues to do with time management and how to beat procrastination. The chapter also discusses quitting your PhD if you want out. Chapter Five addresses important technical aspects of the PhD, such as methodology and referencing, examination, keeping a diary and publishing in a peer reviewed journal. Chapter Six reveals my own reflections on finally finishing my PhD, and Chapter Seven summarises the key lessons I learned from the PhD process.

Chapter One summary

The key purpose of this book is to make you think about the big issues related to doing a PhD. The book is largely based on the author's own reflections and experience. The book is for anyone interested in knowing more about doing a PhD, or indeed, anyone who wishes to know more about goal achievement in general. The chapter defines what a PhD is. As you read about the author's reflections of doing the PhD in this book, you are reminded that hindsight bias may make the events that occurred more predictable than they actually were.

Chapter Two

What it takes to get a PhD

"There is a ruinous misconception that a PhD must be smart. This can't be true. A smart person would know better than to get a PhD."

- Matt Might

Costs involved in earning a PhD

There are a number of costs associated with doing a PhD in addition to the more obvious financial cost. *Opportunity cost* can be defined as the loss of other alternatives when one alternative is chosen. When you are putting your time, energy and resources into one thing then you will not have the same time, energy and resources to do the other thing. The value of the thing that you didn't do is the *opportunity cost*. Consider all the opportunity costs of your decisions; if you do that you will make better use of resources at your disposal. Looking at these costs, the big question which you must answer for yourself is whether or not getting a PhD is worth it for you. Whether to get a PhD or not demands a cost-benefit analysis. In my own case I put very little analysis of future prospects/benefits and costs associated with doing a PhD. I did not stop and think enough, did not explore *Why* enough. I almost drifted into my PhD. What I have written in this chapter in hindsight is what I should have considered before embarking on my PhD journey.

Financial cost

In monetary terms the cost of doing a PhD varies from one university to another and one country to another. You have university fees to pay, research costs and living expenses. These costs can amount to a considerable amount of money each year. You may have to pay more in university fees if you are a foreign student. It is important that you estimate all the annual costs associated with doing a PhD and draw up a budget. Looking at my own budget, I had estimated it would take me three years to complete my PhD, but it actually took me six years! Once my financial support ran out I was forced to take on the additional costs on my own, which was a heavy burden to bear considering I have a wife and three children to support. I also had to contend with rising university fees over the duration of my PhD. In the final years costs had risen sharply due to government budget cutbacks and so called 'austerity.' According to Prospects, the UK's official graduate careers website, the PhD fees in the UK are usually between £3,000 and £6,000 per year ($4,857-$9,714 per annum). Overseas students can expect to pay considerably more. You then have to add to that the cost of maintenance and other related research costs. Depending on where you want to study you may expect fees to increase over time due to economic difficulties. In the USA, according to FindAPHD (http://www.findaphd.com/), the annual cost of doing a PhD is US $28,000-40,000 per year. A key question is, how will you be able to afford the cost of doing a PhD? Do you have a scholarship or financial support? In the USA students routinely take out loans to complete higher education, and the total student debt in the USA recently exceeded USD $1 trillion.

I was fortunate to have had financial support; without this support I would not have been able to do a PhD. It may not be worth going too much into debt to get a PhD. Will you be able to earn additional money as a result of your PhD to pay back your loan? (See Chapter Five—Earning potential of people with PhDs—for a discussion on this topic). Karen Kelsky, a former academic who provides advice to PhD students through her site 'The Professor Is In,' conducted a PhD debt survey in 2014. Some of the survey respondents had racked up so much debt that they are unlikely to be able to pay it off in their lifetime. See http://theprofessorisin.com/ph-d-debt-survey/ to read their individual stories.

Time cost with Family and Friends

When doing a PhD you need to prepare to walk around for years with a monkey on your back—the thesis/your unfinished PhD hanging over you like the Sword of Damocles. There is a cost to be paid in giving up time spent with loved ones and family. Forget the nine-to-five work hours; you have to work long hours to get a PhD. You need to keep working after working hours are over. You also have to give up much of your weekends and holiday time. When you have to lock yourself in a room to research and write a thesis you will likely feel guilty about not having time for loved ones. In particular, if you have young children you are not going to have as much time as you would want to spend with them and take them places weekends etc. as you struggle to make progress with your PhD. As a family man who pursued a PhD, I am very conscious of this cost. If I was not doing a PhD I would have had more time and money to take my children places weekends and on family holidays. I might have had more time to take them to activities like sports and music. Perhaps they would be involved in more sports and activities now if I had never done a PhD. There is also a cost to be paid in terms of your other relationships—friends, spouse or partner—you will have less time for the key people in your life over a number of years, which is a significant cost to be considered.

Myers (1999) talks of two types of stress when working on the PhD dissertation: stress in the social sense and stress in the task sense. Stress in the social sense is brought about when the student is unable to socialise and relax with family, friends, and significant others without feeling guilty that time is being wasted that could be spent working on the PhD. Stress in the task sense is brought about because the amount of time spent working on the PhD makes the researcher feel negligent in terms of time away from family, friends and significant others. These stress factors can lead candidates to drop out of their PhD.

Earnings forgone

When you are doing a PhD all your thoughts, focus and efforts will go to the PhD. The PhD will fill your mind and time and prevent you from doing other things. There are only so many hours in the day! When you are busy doing a PhD you will not be doing paid work. You could have been putting your time instead into something that would generate money. You must factor in the cost of lost earnings. This certainly happened to me as I had to turn down paid consultancy work because I had a PhD deadline to meet. The amount foregone mounts up over a number of years. I might have saved that money for a rainy day, saved for retirement, gone on holidays or invested it in a business. As a parent and married man that money that I lost out on denied my family and I opportunities. Perhaps I could have invested that money in my children in music lessons or trained them to swim etc. Now your loved ones have lost out, too! For me that is a hard cost to swallow. As a parent you cannot get back that time and opportunity for your children. They may very well spend a significant portion of their childhood while you have your head buried in books slaving away for the PhD.

Even if you are relatively young—in your early to mid-twenties—and have transferred straight from being an undergraduate, you will likely be formally and administratively treated as a "student." This has major consequences for your life at a time when a cohort your age is earning well, possibly investing in mortgages, having children and developing a solid career base. According to the Irish Universities Association (2004), you as a doctoral student will likely be:

- Struggling to survive on a meagre student grant if you are lucky to get one.

- Treated as a "student" by legal, tax and social welfare systems.

- Unsure of your rights as a doctoral student. The doctoral student—or the funding agency on the student's behalf—pays the university fees for undertaking doctoral studies: a prima face contract between the student and university for the provision of services to the student. However, the obligations and nature of the services sometimes remain largely unstated.

- Facing an uncertain career path. Save for the very best, career paths are not clearly evident for most doctoral students.

Who could you become if you invested your time elsewhere rather than doing a PhD? Be aware of what you are giving up to do a PhD.

Other opportunity costs

Think of all the other opportunity costs of your doing a PhD. Think of all the things you would like to do—travel the world, start a family etc.—that will have to be put on hold as you pursue your PhD. The average age at the time of graduation for doctoral graduates is 33 years in North America (O'shaughnessy, 2012). This gives a portrayal of students studying well into the time in their lives when they would also be considering engaging in other important life events, such as starting a family, purchasing a home etc. What will you have to give up while you pursue your PhD?

Intelligence and the PhD

Contrary to what many people may think, a PhD is not intellectually hard, but it definitely demands self-discipline and endurance. You don't have to be the most intelligent person in your year to do a PhD. Above a certain minimum level of intelligence, other factors become much more important, such as hard work, persistence and good study habits. All you have to be to do a PhD is to be intelligent enough. According to Wendy Stock et al., (2009) in a paper titled 'Completing an Economics PhD in Five Years,' there are many considerations unique to individual students and faculty which influence completion rates. Some of these are ambition, motivation, persistence, organisational skills, the creativity of students, and interest in students' success as well as mentoring and motivational skills among the university staff.

Frankly, in my experience, a PhD is a test of endurance and hard work more than anything else. Both of these qualities are very important to success with any endeavour, including a PhD. If you stick through all the frustrations and keep working at your PhD then you will get there in the end. In my opinion a PhD is certainly not a measure of intelligence. Looking back now I believe that perhaps I had a limiting belief about my own intelligence. A limiting belief is where we have been conditioned to a certain way of thinking and believe that we cannot achieve beyond a certain limit. We underestimate our own intelligence and we overestimate the intelligence of others—as a result, we sell ourselves short.

I certainly believed that from an intelligence point of view that if I could do a PhD then most people could, as I consider myself of average intelligence. I believe that I am no genius and I still find topics such as statistics difficult to understand even having completed my PhD. As proof of this—and that I am not just pretending—I did a pretty poor Leaving Certificate (end of secondary school exam in Ireland). I did an exam that is best forgotten; in fact, when writing this book I ordered a copy of my results and it felt a little scary, as I had not looked at them since 1985. I had conveniently lost them! In my Leaving Certificate examination I only got one 'honour,' which was a B in economics. In my first degree—an agricultural science degree—I received a 2.2 honour's degree, which is from 50.00 - 59.99%. This is classed as a lower second class (2.2) honours or a US grade B. I notice that Greg Foley, in his book, *The Education Conundrum*, says of someone with a 2.2 "probably does not have the ability to work to PhD level" (in my case I proved Greg Foley wrong!). As you can see from the above, I am not deceiving you when I say that on the face of it I am an average student from an intelligence perspective.

However, I want to make the point that I believe that I am not defined by the above results. For my Leaving Certificate I worked hard and was too stressed to perform well in the exam. I know this because I did a very good matriculation exam shortly afterwards, which gave me more than enough points to enter University. For my Agricultural Science degree I don't remember working very hard or being that organised in my study. In other words, I had the ability to do much better than I did. I believe we all have the potential to do much better if we know how. If we focus our thoughts on 'am I intelligent?' then that is a distraction from getting on with the task at hand. If you think you are not intelligent then this can be self-fulfilling—you don't study because you are stupid anyway—and then what happens? You get poor results, which reinforces your idea that you are not intelligent!

In my own experience doing the PhD did not make me feel more intelligent either. Certainly at times it made me feel more insecure about my own intellectual ability as I interacted with (some) really bright academics. As a PhD student you cannot hide—you are under the spotlight. When you are in an undergraduate programme or master's degree programme where you are part of a large group, you are just one student of many. As a PhD student you can't hide at the back of the class; the spotlight is on you with all your faults and failings. This gives you a feeling of vulnerability. This is scary—you can feel degraded with all your faults and failings exposed to your supervisor(s). This was very uncomfortable for me. I was the guy who liked to hide down at the back of the class, but suddenly I was now on stage. This is when your inner critic can mug you: "You are stupid, you are not smart enough, you are not good enough to do a PhD…"

What I learned is that it is important is to have a *growth mindset*. In other words, to believe that human beings can change and grow and learn new things and can even increase and enhance their learning ability and intelligence through dedication and hard work. This view creates a love of learning and a resilience that is necessary for achievement. I recommend a book by Stanford University psychologist Carol Dweck (2006), called *Mindset*, which explains the growth mindset and its opposite, the fixed mindset. What I am saying is that your attitude is more important than intelligence. In a fixed mindset, people believe their basic qualities—like their intelligence or talent—are simply fixed traits. They spend their time documenting their intelligence or talents instead of developing them. They also believe that talent alone creates success—without effort. I realise now that I had a fixed mindset about my own intelligence and ability and struggled with a limiting belief around my own intelligence. However, I want to make a really important point here that this kind of thinking is a complete time waster! Every thought along the lines of 'Am I smart enough to do this PhD?' takes you away from progressing your PhD, wastes your time and mental energy and holds you back. It's like trying to drive a car with the handbrake on. Therefore, it is really important to develop a growth mindset and not waste time with 'Am I smart enough?' What really matters is not how much intelligence you have but how you use what you do have.

"A child does not need a lightning-fast mind to be a scientist, nor does he need a miraculous memory, nor is it necessary that he get very high grades in school. The only point that counts is that the child have a high degree of interest in science."

– Dr. Edward Teller, Physicist

Grit

Grit, or the ability to stick with it (staying power) and endure failure, is far more important than intelligence. Angela Lee Duckworth describes grit as a tenacious, dogged perseverance, and she gives an informative talk about grit on TED (see: http://www.youtube.com/watch?v=qaeFnxSfSC4).

Grit is a characteristic that you see in famous scientists/inventors such as Thomas Edison. When you read about the life of Edison you learn that he was really determined and passionate. He kept at it and at it until he made a breakthrough in whatever he was working on. When performing scientific research, one is unsurprisingly confronted with unknown territory. This means that failures are inevitable. Resilience (or resiliency) is our ability to adapt and bounce back when things don't go as planned. Resilient people don't wallow or dwell on failures; they acknowledge the situation, learn from their mistakes, and then move forward. Being resilient means that when we do fail, we bounce back, we have the strength to learn the lessons we need to learn, and we can move on to bigger and better things. My own PhD supervisor would from time to time say to me "we are where we are." It's like saying, okay, it would be better if we had made more progress but let us accept where we are now and get on with it—in other words back to work! That's a winning attitude.

Staying power is really important if you want to succeed in getting a PhD. The drop-out rate for PhDs is high. According to an article in the Guardian newspaper (2012) in the United States, only 57% of PhD students obtained their PhD ten years after enrolment. In the humanities, the figure dropped to 49%. In the Netherlands, as monitored by the 'Association of Dutch Universities' (VSNU), between 2001 and 2009, the average duration of a PhD is five years (VSNU, 2011). In the US a PhD takes much longer and depends on your subject area. Maldonado et al. (2013) cite a 2006 US study which found that seven years was the median time required to complete a doctorate in the US in the life sciences, 12.7 years in education, and 9.7 in the humanities. In order to get your PhD you must put in a lot of effort and get very little reward for years.

According to Brian Martin, physicist turned social science professor, persistence is also the key to successful publication in academic journals. Having articles rejected and being able to learn from that is key—far more important than factors such as intelligence. Donald Hall, in his book *The Academic Self*, recommends that experienced academics tell more about their failures as encouragement to others to not give up. When you see academic articles published, books written and PhDs completed, you do not see the struggles and failures and dogged persistence over a long period of time associated with getting to that stage. When you then experience failure and rejection of your work you may not know that this is very much part of the process. You have to be able to stick with it—iterate, learn, improve—but most of all, stick with it and keep at it. The question is, are you ready to put in the effort? Are you willing to pay the price in terms of effort required to get your PhD?

> *"Understand that failure is not the opposite of success. Failure is an essential part of success. Once you succeed, no one will remember your failures anyway..."*
>
> *- Steve Pavlina*

Hard work

I have mentioned hard work a lot already. However, this is really important and needs to be stressed again. If you want to get your PhD you simply have to work hard at it. The harder you work at it the quicker you will complete it. Greg Foley, in his book, *The Education Conundrum,* stresses the importance of student commitment and simply putting in the time needed. You simply have to work hard. Greg makes an analogy with a professional sports person: there is a limit on how much fun a professional sports person can have when practicing; they simply have to put in the effort and time. In the same way, learning much of the time is hard work and often boring. Much of the time doing a PhD is also hard work and boring. You just have to knuckle down and get on with it. You will, of course, experience moments of great insight when you finally understand some concept or other. However, to get to these points you have to put in the effort.

Motivation and getting a PhD

I am certainly no intellectual genius—just an ordinary guy who likes learning new things and who did a PhD. The title PhD after my name on the front of this book looks great, and I am proud of that achievement. I really feel that I deserve it. It represents years of toil and labour and years of sacrifice. To me it is proof that I can persist and that I have the discipline to achieve big goals. However, I could have chosen a different goal. For example, I could have chosen to run my own business and generate a certain amount of money. I could have chosen to become wealthy as my goal and aimed to live in a big house, go on nice holidays etc. If you wish to become wealthy then start a business! I could have invested my time and energy elsewhere other than in doing a PhD. Questions I must ask myself now are: What motivated me to do a PhD? Also, was the PhD goal a good goal to set for myself and was it worth the six years of effort I spent on it? These are really important questions.

Regarding the first question on my motivation for doing a PhD, I think there are multiple reasons. I became interested in the idea of doing a PhD towards the end of my first master's degree in environmental resource management in 1993. I was offered a place on a PhD programme in Wales, which I couldn't take up at the time, but it really attracted me to continued study. For my master's degree I was working on a mini thesis on bee morphology. The PhD place I was offered was also related to bees, my passion at the time. I did not have the finances at that stage to do the PhD. I think at some level the idea of doing a

PhD stuck in the back of my mind, and years later in the mid-2000s and living in Kenya, I still had an interest in doing a PhD. At that point of my life I had more free time to study and thought a PhD would be a good idea to keep myself occupied. I had just completed a second master's degree by distance learning and felt that I could go further with my studies. I wanted to achieve a difficult goal which would stretch me. Doing a PhD was like climbing Mount Everest for me—a very difficult goal to set and achieve. To me doing a PhD was a personal 'Big Hairy Audacious Goal' (BHAG). The term BHAG was proposed by James Collins and Jerry Porras in their 1994 book, *Built to Last: Successful Habits of Visionary Companies*. A BHAG encourages companies to define visionary goals that are more strategic and emotionally compelling. On a personal level BHAG's are goals that are big, exciting, scary, and get you out of your comfort zone (another BHAG I am toying with at the moment is to run a marathon—a pretty big, exciting and scary goal for me as I am overweight at the moment!).

On reflection I also believe that I did a PhD out of a feeling that I needed to prove something to myself, and I suspect this feeling was born out of low self-esteem. I felt that I needed the PhD certificate to prove something. That feeling of needing to prove something to myself may go back to my childhood. I needed to prove to myself that I was smart enough to do it. However, what I have found is that at the end of a PhD I do not feel any smarter. I needed to deal with the underlying issue, which in my case was perhaps low self-esteem, and doing a PhD did not solve the problem.

I also started my PhD because I thought it would be a nice thing to do in the sense that I wanted to learn new things, become an expert in my field and contribute to the development of new knowledge. I was interested in exploring my topic and pushing the bounds of knowledge. To some extent I also enjoyed research and learning new things. I wanted to do a PhD because of the love of learning—education for its own sake.

There is also the issue of status seeking behaviour. At a subconscious level perhaps I was seeking status through the PhD. Boosting my ego was part of my motivation for doing a PhD. This is something that has just occurred to me when writing this book. I think at some level I wanted to boost my ego and be called 'Doctor.' It sounds great to be called 'Doctor' and the associated respect that is implied. Having a higher status is something attractive to most of us at some level. I was living in Kenya at the time of starting my PhD, where people have a lot of deference for PhD holders. I also think universities appeal to our perception of status when marketing their PhDs.

Greg Foley, in his book, *The Education Conundrum,* makes the observation that when academically weak students come back from work placements they often return with very good reports from their employer. There appears to be an assumption in society that everyone should move up the education ladder. That we should move from bachelor's degree to master's degree to PhD, and the higher we go up the ladder the better we are. But should we? Does having a PhD make me better at my job? Probably not.

We can examine motivation to do a PhD in relation to Maslow's hierarchy of needs. In his influential paper of 1943, 'A Theory of Human Motivation,' the American psychologist Abraham Maslow proposed that healthy human beings have a certain number of needs, and that these needs are arranged in a hierarchy, with some needs (such as physiological and safety needs) being more primitive or basic than others. I believe that my main motivation for doing the PhD was a more basic ego need such as self-esteem and recognition. Perhaps I could have achieved this need in other less taxing ways without doing a PhD!

In general I thought it would be a good idea to do a PhD without really knowing what doing a PhD entailed. On reflection I see that I had both conscious and sub-conscious motivations to do a PhD. The conscious motivations for doing a PhD were the logical reasons I have given above, such as wanting to use my time well and add to knowledge in my field, and the sub-conscious motivations were low self-esteem and status seeking behaviour—which I was not really aware of at the time. I realise now that I did not spend enough time thinking through my motivation for wanting a PhD. I did not think enough before starting. Perhaps I would be a lot better off today if I had thought it through better. Perhaps I should have never done a PhD—perhaps it was the wrong path for me. This is the second question: Was the PhD goal a good goal to set for myself and was it worth the six years of effort I spent on it? The answer to this question is personal to my own particular circumstance, and I am struggling to answer this question throughout this book.

An important question that you should ask yourself is: Why do you want to do a PhD? What really motivates you? You are thinking of embarking on something that can change your life, either for better or worse, and you really need to think this decision through properly. Take yourself forward in time to your graduation day. There you are with PhD in hand—now what next? It is important to have a clear vision of what you want and what is motivating you to do a PhD.

Good reasons to do a PhD

When I was looking at this issue of motivation I found that candidates applying for a PhD position in Germany are often asked to submit a letter of motivation, also called a "statement of purpose." The statement of purpose is also commonly used in the United States as part of the admissions process to graduate school. Whether or not you are required to do this, you need to write your own "statement of purpose" for yourself. Make sure you are comfortable with the answers to questions below:

- ✓ What are your professional goals? Which sector would you like to work in after obtaining your PhD?

- ✓ Why are you applying for this specific PhD position? Which aspect of the position or research topic is especially interesting to you and/or beneficial in pursuing your professional goals?

- ✓ How does the PhD position fit into your academic background?

- ✓ Why do you think you are the right person for this position?

- ✓ Have you already gained professional/scientific experience relevant to this position?

- ✓ How could you best apply your knowledge and acquired skills to this position?

- ✓ How could the institution (or organisation), to which you are applying, benefit by selecting you, and what could you contribute to the project or programme? Try to put yourself in the employer's position and avoid writing in the first-person only.

It is worth spending some time to consider the above questions even if it is not a requirement for you. It is important that you have a clear understanding of your own motivation for doing a PhD. Time invested now is well worth it before you spend years of your life toiling on a PhD.

Areas which I believe are some worthy reasons to do a PhD:

- ✓ Do it if you love research and have a particular aptitude and interest in research.

- ✓ You want to pursue an academic career and have clear and realistic career goals in relation to getting a job in academia. 'Realistic' is the important point here, as an academic job is not easy to come by. For example, an article in the *Economist* magazine titled 'The Disposable Academic' (December 16, 2010), reported that America produced more than 100,000 doctoral degrees between 2005 and 2009. In the same period there were just 16,000 new professorships.

- ✓ You want to become more intellectually engaged with and more critically sophisticated in the study of some issue or field.

- ✓ You want a PhD to demonstrate your competence at research. However, you do not need a PhD to do good research. You can conduct good research, write a peer reviewed paper and publish in a respected journal all without a PhD.

Personality and getting a PhD

According to an article in the Guardian newspaper (2012), a PhD, especially in the humanities, is a lonely affair. I would certainly concur with that. Doing a PhD requires long hours at the computer away from people, writing, reading etc. Since I am naturally an introverted person I had no problem with that at all. My Myers-Briggs personality type is INFJ—Introvert, iNtuitive, Feeling, Judging. I believe self-awareness is very important in order to understand yourself and your own personality traits. If you are an extroverted person you would need strategies to recharge your batteries through the company of others. It should be remembered that getting a PhD also involves dealing with the personalities of others and particularly of your supervisor(s). Self-awareness and sensitivity to the personalities of others is very important. According to Boom et al. (2013), personality characteristics that supervisors highly valued in their PhD-candidates were related to the ability to work in a team, while at the same time also being able to work independently and autonomously. Openness for receiving feedback and criticism, self-reflection, and enthusiasm were also seen as important individual characteristics that supervisors valued in PhD candidates. Thus, both the ability to stand on one's own two feet when needed while also being receptive to feedback were found to be important.

Two personality types in the PhD candidates were considered a problem to the PhD process. One was a candidate that was too independent, overconfident, not being open for criticism and having difficulties accepting authority and expertise of the supervisor. The other concerned candidates who were too dependent, passive, waiting for solutions offered and having no self-confidence. Being either too sloppy or too perfectionist can also be a problem. I had the latter problem, which resulted in my being afraid to share my work with my supervisor out of fear that it would not be good enough. I was scared of being vulnerable—when you share your work with someone you will be vulnerable. You need to have the courage to embrace vulnerability. This fear of criticism slowed me down until I learned to openly share drafts and not be such a perfectionist. You need to learn to embrace constructive criticism as an academic and to seek it out. In the beginning I did not know this and ran away from an avoided criticism. To find out more on vulnerability there are some very informative talks on the internet by Brené Brown, a US researcher who researches topics such as vulnerability, courage, worthiness, and shame—which I recommend you watch (see References and Useful Resources at the end of the book). Understanding why you may fear vulnerability and that you are not alone in feeling this can help progress your PhD a lot quicker as you learn to seek out feedback on your work and not be afraid of feeling vulnerable.

Skills and knowledge

In addition to grit mentioned earlier, learning the skills needed to be a good academic is also very important, such as critical thinking, research methods, data analysis and good academic writing. However, you can build these skills over time. These skills are learnable. You can learn these skills by taking classes, interacting with your supervisor and reading and applying what you learn. Once you have the motivation and grit to keep working at your PhD you will learn these research skills. Self-awareness in areas that you are particularly weak is useful, as you can then seek additional courses to build skills and knowledge on particular subjects.

The support of others

Having the support of others during the PhD process is vital. In particular, you need the support of close family, such as your parents or your spouse/partner. The PhD process becomes very hard without this support and it is important to keep family and friends onside. At the end of the day your PhD is a burden to all your close family and friends, and they will all pay the price of your PhD as well. For example, your time with them will be limited, with evenings and weekends given up to research and thesis writing. Even when taking a break with them it will be hard to avoid thinking about the PhD. As mentioned earlier, there will also be opportunity costs of earnings foregone while doing the PhD and the possible additional burden of research costs and university fees etc. I was fortunate that I did have the support of my wife and children in doing the PhD; however, I was also aware that the burden of my studies was impacting their lives as well as my own. Earnings foregone affected them as well. Money paid to the university in fees or other PhD related expenses was a burden shared by the whole family.

Chapter Two summary

Doing a PhD can be costly in financial terms; however, you must also be aware of other costs such as earnings foregone while doing the PhD as well as the reduced time and attention available for your loved ones. The decision to embark on a PhD or not requires a thorough cost-benefit analysis.

In order to get a PhD you do not need to be intellectually brilliant but you do need dogged determination and persistence to keep going for years with little reward for your efforts. Given that you are going to devote years of your life to this goal, you must be sure this is the correct goal for you. Self-awareness and sensitivity to the personalities of others is very important. Openness to receiving feedback and enthusiasm are also very important personal traits, while skills and knowledge related to research can be learned. The support of others, such as close family, is really important as they are also paying a price for your PhD through earnings foregone or your reduced time availability.

Chapter Three

Getting Started With Your PhD

"The secret of getting ahead is getting started."

- Mark Twain

Choosing a PhD programme

My thinking as a prospective student was that if I am lucky I will get a college to take me in and I will be lucky to be offered a PhD place and I will be lucky to get a PhD supervisor! Bull—with this type of thinking you will not get the best deal for yourself. Put yourself in the driving seat—you select them first. They need students. It's a bit like job hunting: at interview you always have the power to select them first. You get to choose them first—you choose who to apply to. You are not going with cap in hand—*please take me*. If you are competing to be accepted then know why; why are they so good —a particularly good supervisor, a particularly good programme in high demand with good career prospects? Do your background research. You need to be aware that we live in a world where education is more and more a commodity to be bought and sold. Institutions of higher learning are adopting a business model and becoming more like corporations, as discussed by Mary Gallagher in her book, *Academic Armageddon: An Irish Requiem for Higher Education*. As a prospective student you are the potential consumer and you need to make the right choices for you and not just be sold on a particular institution because of their convincing sales pitch. You have to be able to look deeper than the glossy brochures with pictures of handsome students studiously examining test tubes etc. PhDs from prestigious research universities may be perceived as better. PhDs earned under the supervision of noted researchers may also be perceived as more valuable. In Europe, PhDs from older, more prestigious universities are perceived as worth more than those from newer ones. An important point would be to choose a university with expertise in your field of study and a good potential supervisor. Selecting a good supervisor is very important as will be discussed later in this chapter. You need also to be aware of the different kinds of PhDs on offer in North America and Europe as outlined in the next section.

Varieties of PhD programmes

An important point to keep in mind is that the structure of all PhDs is not the same. For example, in the USA students mostly start with a period of two years of course work (foundation courses and domain specific courses). Most doctoral programmes in the United States require that the students pass exams after all the required courses, after which they need to defend a dissertation proposal. They can then enter the stage of 'candidacy' (2nd stage), i.e. a permission for them to begin working on their dissertation. Most students will enter this stage at the 3rd or 4th year of their doctoral studies (though this varies across disciplines). Another fundamental structural difference between PhD programmes at European and North American (Canada and United States) universities is that the latter typically integrate master's level studies, which means that a PhD candidate may, in some cases, obtain a master's degree en route to the doctoral degree. In European universities students tend to complete a master's before progressing to a PhD. As they integrate master's degrees, PhD programmes in North America take longer. PhDs also vary within Europe, and in the European Union, doctoral studies are now coming under the "Bologna Process"—an attempt to develop a level of commonality and mutual recognition for different national doctoral systems across the EU.

The traditional Irish model of PhD education could be described as being similar to the "apprenticeship model," where lone or small groups of students are situated within a single higher education institution. The primary focus is towards their PhD thesis, and if they receive any transferable skills training then this is an "extra" and not part of their core training (ACSTI, 2009). This was the model of PhD education which I received. Some European universities are now offering their students structured PhDs, including training in skills such as communication and teamwork, which are aimed at being useful in the labour market. In Britain, for example, a four-year 'New Route PhD' claims to develop just such skills in graduates. Similar to

Britain, Ireland's Strategy for Science Technology and Innovation (SSTI) promotes the development of 'structured programmes' where students take courses to develop skills such as project management, time management, team working and communication skills. The student can also study specialist modules that are of direct relevance to their particular PhD project. The focus is still on the PhD thesis and contributing a unique body of knowledge, but the generic and transferable skills are embedded in student's education and training. Doing advanced modules in their discipline, especially in subjects directly related to a student's project, is the norm in the USA.

Demark has developed another type of PhD known as the Industrial PhD programme. The Industrial PhD programme began in 1970 and the student earns their PhD in collaboration with enterprise. The programme is targeted at master's level students and businesses that can professionally support a three year business-oriented research and development project. The Industrial PhD programme accounts for about 7% of all PhD graduates in Denmark and the target has now been raised to 10%. The main aims of the programme are to:

- ✓ Up skill researchers working in enterprise;

- ✓ Build know-how, knowledge dissemination and interaction between academic and research institutions and enterprises.

- ✓ Ensure commercialisation of new know-how and research, including development of knowledge and technology based enterprises.

As demonstrated in this section, not all PhD programmes are the same and you need to understand the structure of the PhD programme you are interested in doing. You are the customer. Ask yourself, will the programme allow you to develop the skills you need to make you more attractive to future employers? Will the programme give you a broad range of skills in addition to your specific research topic?

University rankings

Another factor to be aware of when choosing a university to do your PhD with is the world rankings of universities. There are three big international indices:

- ✓ Shanghai: http://www.shanghairanking.com/
- ✓ Times Higher Education: http://www.timeshighereducation.co.uk/world-university-rankings/
- ✓ QS: http://www.topuniversities.com/qs-world-university-rankings

For those interested in United Kingdom universities there is the Guardian University Guide:

http://www.theguardian.com/education/table/2013/jun/03/university-league-table-2014.

Apparently, people are using the guide. The University of Surrey found that its applications increased by 1/3 when its numbers went up in the rankings.

A criticism of the rankings is that they all measure different things. One focuses on reputation among business people, for example, while another concentrates on the scale of published research in the sciences. Also, the criteria used for each index change regularly, along with the pool of institutions examined. However, the indices can give you an indication of the quality of the institution in comparison with others.

Financing your PhD

As discussed in Chapter Two, this is a really important issue. Is it possible to get funding to do your PhD? I had funding and would not have been able to do the PhD without financial support. The bulk of my own PhD costs were paid for. Because I went on longer than expected working at my PhD (I had support for three years and finished in six years), I had to use my own money and that was hard. However, lack of finance pushed me to complete in the end, especially as the university drastically increased fees and I had no option but to knuckle down or drop out. I also worked throughout my PhD. It was very hard to serve two masters—work on my PhD and my job. An important point here is to have enough funding to allow you to avoid the potential distraction of full-time work and to be able to focus on your doctoral study.

On the positive side, I completed my PhD relatively debt free (I had to borrow on my credit card towards the end to keep going). Just as well I did not rake up too much debt as so far there is no lucrative job at the end of the PhD, and I am currently earning the average industrial wage in Ireland. This wage allows me to pay the mortgage and bills—but not much else.

According to Peter Fiske in an article in *Nature* titled "What is a PhD really worth?" (Fiske, 2011), raking up debt is not worth it. No programme of higher education can guarantee its graduates gainful and lucrative employment. At best, a graduate programme in any discipline can provide its students with key skills, knowledge and abilities. How the graduates apply that learning is up to them. In other words, when you complete your PhD there is no guarantee that the qualification will guarantee you a lucrative job. Do you really want to live frugally for years as a PhD student, rake up debt and then emerge at the end of the process and find that you cannot find a well-paying job? It is therefore well worth the effort involved to search for a scholarship to finance your PhD.

Choosing your subject

Choose your subject for PhD research carefully and choose a topic that you will be able to use and enjoy working on. Take a long-term perspective—project yourself ten to twenty years into the future. Where do you want to be and what do you want to be doing in ten years' time? Write out a description of your ideal life ten and twenty years into the future. This inevitably develops a longer-time perspective. I know this is difficult, but it is important to—at the very least—try.

In 1974, sociologist Dr. Edward Banfield of Harvard University wrote a book titled, *The Unheavenly City*." He described one of the most insightful studies on success and priority setting ever conducted. Banfield's goal was to find out how and why some people became financially independent during the course of their working lifetimes. He found that taking a longer term perspective was key.

Stephen Covey in his book, *The 7 Habits of Highly Successful People,* reminds us that "If the ladder is not leaning against the right wall, every step we take just gets us to the wrong place faster..." You don't want to study something for years and realise later that this is not for you. You are going to spend a number of years of your precious life (and you only get one) studying a topic for your PhD—what then? Apart from enjoyment you also need to consider employment prospects and earning potential. Research by O'Leary and Sloane (2005) in Britain showed that the financial returns from doing a PhD depend on the area studied. The research showed that obtaining a higher degree benefits women more than men in earning potential. PhDs in medicine, sciences, business and finance and (for men only) engineering significantly enhance productivity. PhDs in social sciences, languages and arts do not enhance earnings significantly for either sex.

In Ireland it is government policy to substantially increase the stock of PhD graduates in order that it contributes to the development of a 'Knowledge Economy' also known as the 'Smart Economy.' PhD education is seen as a driver for innovation in enterprise. However, as we have seen, not all PhDs are the same and some PhDs are much more marketable than others.

We need to be careful of the problem of silent evidence. In other words, we only hear about success—we only hear about people who go on to have great careers after doing a PhD, while we hear nothing of people with PhDs for which their PhD does not enhance their career.

Investigate and think well before starting your PhD. In hindsight, I should have given a lot more thought to the subject area of my PhD. I should have foreseen that I might have to leave Kenya and Africa at some point and that my expertise would then be pretty useless once I had left. I completed my

PhD on African beekeeping development and there is not much demand for my expertise in Ireland! No killer bees here or particular need for my particular expertise. If I had carried out my PhD research on dairy cows, for example, there would be a great demand in Ireland for my expertise! In hindsight, I should have really given this more thought when choosing my topic for research. Yes, I really like what I studied, but perhaps I should have worked on a subject area where I could more easily have found demand for my expertise outside Kenya/Africa.

However, I have two minds on this issue—follow your own passion regardless of how marketable your subject area is and see where it leads, or, be more pragmatic and calculating. The choice is always yours; my main point is to think it through as best you can before you decide your research subject. Look ahead to the end of your PhD and what you might do afterwards with your PhD. My overall advice is to focus on an area of study for your PhD which you are really interested in but which is also marketable to potential employers or will allow you to make a lucrative self-employed income, perhaps as a consultant.

Long term personal planning

"Begin with the end in mind."

- Stephen Covey

If you are unsure where your interests and passions lie, I recommend an excellent book by Richard Nelson Bolles called *What Color is Your Parachute* (Ten Speed Press). There are many detailed exercises in the book which are worth doing in order to get a clearer picture of your interests and what you would really like to work at. You need to reconcile your desire to do a PhD with the direction in which the exercises are pointing you in. Perhaps a PhD is completely unnecessary for you to get into the career of choice that the exercises are pointing you towards. If so, then do not do the PhD—there is no point! You have just saved yourself years of frustration and a lot of money!

One of the things that prevented me from taking a long term perspective was my own thoughts such as, 'I am not good enough to get a PhD' or 'I will likely drop out along the way.' These thoughts are useless and distracting. If you never really believe that you will finish the PhD and are distracted by these types of thoughts then it is hard to think what will happen post completion of the PhD. Don't get trapped by the thought—'well, I don't know if I will be able to finish the PhD, so I will think about careers after I finish.' Assume that all goes well and you finish the PhD—you need to know which direction the PhD is taking you. If you follow the advice in this book and keep working steadily at your PhD <u>you will</u> complete it. Visualise yourself with your PhD completed and be clear what you want to do afterwards. Base your decisions on thorough research on yourself, your interests and likely career prospects for your chosen subject area. You are going to come out after years of study with a PhD in your chosen field. What will you do with your expertise? Where do you want to work? Will the demand be there in the future for your expertise?

We live in a rapidly changing world. Will the demand for your services/expertise likely increase or decrease in the future? It is certainly a very useful exercise to look into the future and get a short (1-5 years), medium (5-10 years) and longer term (greater than 10 years) perspective on the employment prospects for your particular area of expertise/industry. See your PhD as a stepping stone to your chosen career goal rather than an end in itself and you will likely be motivated to complete your PhD much quicker. For me, my PhD was an end in itself without a clear goal on completion. This, I think, contributed to my slow pace and the PhD taking much longer than necessary. Chapter Five discusses the career prospects of PhD graduates in more detail.

Choosing a good Supervisor

"Supervision quality and relationship with the supervisor are considered to be amongst the most important issues for a PhD candidate."

- Boom et al (2013)

According to Gill and Burnard (2008), research has shown that effective supervision can significantly influence the quality of the PhD and its eventual success or failure. The choice of a dissertation chair might be the most important decision in doctoral study (Bair & Haworth, 1999). Findings from a specific study setting (Maastricht University, The Netherlands) suggest that one of the most pronounced reasons for dropout is a personal mismatch between supervisors and PhD candidates (Boom et al., 2013). A good relationship between the PhD candidate and his or her supervisor will not only enhance a candidate's motivation, it might also increase his or her output. The issue of the relationship between supervisor and PhD student draws parallels with other relationships we may have. Therefore, who you choose as your supervisor is a really big deal and can determine before you even start your PhD whether or not you will finish or drop out! Choosing a good supervisor is a hugely important issue and can make or break your PhD! You may have a team of supervisors; however, there will likely be one lead supervisor. According to Tara Brabazon in an article in the Times Higher Education, less is more (Brabazon, 2013). A good relationship with a well-qualified, experienced and committed supervisor will ensure that the PhD candidate will produce a strong thesis with the least delay.

In my own situation I had one main supervisor throughout the PhD process. I also had a committee, but I only met with the committee on a small number of occasions, and one committee member left the University early on in my PhD process. Therefore, I was mostly only dealing with one person. Choose wisely and carefully! Your supervisor will be in a position of power in the relationship. Consciously or subconsciously you will be dependent on the supervisors' judgement, feedback, availability, and approval. The supervisor is in charge and decides when the thesis is ready for submission etc. Difficulties in this key relationship can lead to insecurities on the part of the student. Good communication between student and supervisor is really important to overcome difficulties and solve problems. A good supervisor will have good coaching skills and take the lead when necessary and provide clear direction and keep the project on track to completion. A good supervisor will motivate the PhD student and make the student enthusiastic about their research by showing their own dedication, by being available, providing support, and creating the right atmosphere by inspiring their candidates and making them feel passionate about their research. A good supervisor will enhance the self-confidence and professional development of the PhD candidate.

It is important to find a supervisor who is a good match for you. That means someone who you not only enjoy working with and who works well with you, but someone who is interested in the same sub-specialty of your discipline as you.

Qualities of a good Supervisor

You ought to evaluate your own potential supervisor against the factors listed below. Most importantly, ask his or her past students or current students what he or she is really like.

The characteristics of a good PhD supervisor are:

- ✓ Expertise and interest in your field of study
- ✓ Interested in you and your work
- ✓ A hard worker who takes his/her position seriously and will send you good quality feedback promptly
- ✓ Approachable and friendly
- ✓ Someone who will encourage and motivate
- ✓ Firm but fair
- ✓ Honesty
- ✓ Flexibility
- ✓ A clear thinker
- ✓ Analytical thinking
- ✓ Empathy
- ✓ Being a team player

- ✓ Patience
- ✓ Insightfulness
- ✓ Ability to self-reflect
- ✓ A good communicator
- ✓ Being a good listener

Empathy listed above not only means that supervisors should be able to understand the PhD candidate in work-related situations, but also in private situations, shifting from a role of a supervisor to the role of a colleague. A good supervisor will also take an interest in the PhD candidate as a person and in their private life. A good supervisor will be interested in your research and work. I found that this is very motivating when someone other than yourself is really keen to learn and understand your work.

My experience

In my own case I chose a topic that really interested me and I looked around for a supervisor. A potential supervisor was recommended to me from a prodigious university, and I met with him in Kenya. All seemed fine. He was quite a well-know scientist. I then arranged to visit him at his home for further discussions (he lived in the UK). He had given me directions to his home and I was to get off at a particular bus stop. I was totally new to the area and got off at the wrong stop (but not far from where he had told me). However, he became annoyed and called me 'silly' because I got off at the wrong bus stop. I realised very quickly that if he is getting annoyed and calling me silly now then how about when I actually start the PhD study! This was a man with very little patience, and he was starting to make me feel uncomfortable. I decided that I would not continue with him—thank God! You need a good relationship with a supervisor—you need a friend and mentor who will carry you through the tough times.

After my first attempt at finding a supervisor failed, another person in an Irish university was recommended to me as being good. It turned out that I was lucky that this person was indeed a very good supervisor; however, given the importance of this decision I put very little effort into choosing my PhD supervisor. What I should have done was make a conscious effort to talk with a number of his past and current students to find out more. Given the importance of this decision, I did not approach finding a supervisor systematically.

An unforeseen consequence of my change of supervisor was that the first man was an entomologist and the second was a rural development specialist. This meant that by changing supervisor I effectively changed the whole approach of my PhD. I wanted to study African beekeeping and with the first supervisor I would have studied through a bee biology lens, as he was an entomologist. With the second supervisor I ended up studying bees and livelihoods, which is more from a social science perspective. The decision to change supervisor completely changed my PhD (still on the same overall topic but coming at if from a different angle!). Again, I took that decision to change supervisor with little or no thought. I was more interested in the biological aspect of African bees, but my second supervisor was not an entomologist so I ended up looking at African beekeeping through a completely different lens.

However, once I began my PhD my supervisor always made time for me and my work. Finding a supportive supervisor who would not lose his cool was extremely important to me. I would not have been able to handle it if the relationship had been based on criticism. My PhD supervisor also demonstrated empathy when I moved countries and failed to make progress on my PhD for about a year. He understood how difficult it was to settle back and integrate back into Irish society after living for fifteen years in Africa. I did not fully understand how difficult this transition was at the time and was perhaps too hard on myself when I failed to make progress on my PhD. My supervisor demonstrated great empathy in this regard. He was also always concerned about me as a person and also about my family. He would always enquire about them and how they were doing and settling in Ireland. He was also interested and helpful regarding my career. He was always willing to act as my referee when I was changing jobs and would also alert me to any potential job opportunities which he heard of.

As regards my PhD, he always took an interest in my academic work and gave me very insightful feedback. He was always well prepared when we met, having gone through my work and prepared his feedback thoroughly. He also helped me to set deadlines for myself and plan what needed to done and when my next draft was to be ready. He was always clear and perceptive about what needed to be done. He would schedule regular meetings to review progress. At the times when I failed to meet the deadlines and make progress he was always pragmatic. He would say 'we are where we are' with a focus on how do we move forward from here (no point regretting the past). He never once berated me for not making progress. I learned very quickly that the PhD was my responsibility—he was there to help and support, but I had to get my act together, and I eventually did.

My supervisor was also personally inspiring. He demonstrated personal commitment and hard work. He was very busy but never failed to respond to my work. On the rare occasion when he delayed in giving me feedback on my work he was always very apologetic. This showed he had high standards for himself. My supervisor had a very good reputation within the university and was well respected. He was considered a hard and committed worker by both staff and students. People have described him as a person of high energy. His former students, including his former PhD students, would tell me that he was very thorough. The common refrain was 'If you can get through him, you can get through anyone.' In other words, he had high standards for the work. This is actually very good because when you come to be examined you will not run into problems as your work will be high quality.

I was always able to contact my supervisor—he would respond quickly by email. He also showed a lot of insight/experience later on in my PhD process and before I had written any of my thesis by advising me to publish my work in a peer reviewed journal. Writing a peer reviewed paper was a good strategy towards my completing the thesis. If the work is good enough for a peer reviewed journal then it is good enough to get you a PhD. This goal of publishing in a respected peer reviewed journal captured my imagination and helped propel me forward. Overall, the good working relationship I had with my PhD supervisor was key to my eventual PhD success. You are going to be working closely with your PhD supervisor over a number of years. Make sure you invest sufficient effort to find a good supervisor as outlined in the next section.

How to find a good supervisor

As we have seen, the relationship with your supervisor is a key relationship and you are going to be attached at the hip to this person for years. To save yourself a lot of grief you need to find out some things about your potential supervisor. How long have they been a supervisor and how many PhD students have they supervised? This is really important. Do you want to be the guinea pig and be the first? It is absolutely essential to talk with a potential supervisor's past or current PhD students before making your request. Talk to these students and find out what the supervisor is really like. You want to know what he/she is like on good days and bad days. What are they like to deal with? The supervisor's skills, such as empathy, communication and coaching skills, are highly important for matching or mismatching with a PhD candidate (Delaney, 2008; Gill & Burnard, 2008; Sinclair, 2004).

Understand your supervisor's research background and knowledge in your subject area. In my own case my supervisor's research background and experience was in rural development. My interest was in beekeeping development. By virtue of choosing my supervisor I ended up looking at beekeeping development through a rural development lens. This was not necessarily what I wanted, as I was also deeply interested in bee biology. Therefore, it is very important to understand your potential supervisor's research background and understand which research perspective they are coming from. Read any past research papers or publications they have written. This will give you a good understanding of where their interests lie; you will likely be following a similar research lens if you choose this person as your supervisor.

Knowledge aside, a good supervisor should be willing to devote time to the thesis. Potential supervisors who are great researchers may not be the best teachers. Be careful; don't just look at their track record in research—will they make time for you and support you on your PhD journey? Ask their current or past students. In other words, beware of the elusive professor, however brilliant his or her reputation!

Try to understand your supervisor

Try to put yourself in the shoes of your supervisor and understand where they are coming from. They may also have insecurities and doubts about their own skills and knowledge, in particular if they are new supervisors.

Remember also that there are benefits to your supervisor and the institution in having you register as a PhD student. Your supervisor will expand his or her skills and knowledge in research and your particular subject area by supervising you. Postgraduate students bring in grants and fees for the university and beef up their supervisors' publication records. PhD students can be useful in taking on some of the teaching load of the supervisor.

I did not think of the above benefits to my supervisor and the university. My thoughts were: "Aren't I lucky to be accepted into this PhD programme!" Remember, it's a two way street, and benefits flow both ways. Remember also that you get to choose them (the institution and supervisor) before they choose you and that this is your life we are taking about, so make sure that you are happy before proceeding with your PhD.

Parallels with business

A man called Napoleon Hill, author of the book, *Think and Grown Rich* (first published 1937), advocated setting up what he called a mastermind group. Hill defined a mastermind group as:

"...two or more people who work in perfect harmony for the attainment of a definite purpose..."

By Hill's definition then what you are forming with your PhD supervisor/supervisory team is a mastermind group with the definite aim of achieving your PhD.

In the business world a mastermind group can support you in the following ways:

- You can seek opinions on potential courses of action.

- Your mastermind partner(s) can suggest courses of action that you might not otherwise think of.

- You can use the mastermind as a recurring milestone for the progress.

- You can use the mastermind as a strong enforcer of accountability.

There are clear parallels here with your PhD supervisory team and how it can help you achieve your PhD. According to Hill, for your mastermind group to work you need to be careful to have the right people in it who you can work with and get along with (hence the importance of selecting the right PhD supervisor).

Chapter Three summary

Doing a PhD is a lot tougher than you may think! However, not all PhDs are the same; they vary between institutions and countries. Make sure you are aware of these differences. A PhD is expensive; it's worth making sure that you get your PhD funded. If you take on debt to finance your PhD it may not pay off in the end. Choose a subject which really interests you but also one that you can make use of/will enhance your career prospects after you finish. Take a long-term perspective and consider the likely demand for your expertise on completion of your PhD.

Choose a PhD supervisor with great care. This one decision alone could be the difference between succeeding with your PhD or failure. Evaluate any potential supervisor carefully and determine if you are a good match with this person. Make sure to ask current and past students what this person is really like.

Your supervisor and university/institution also benefit from having you as a PhD student, so make sure that you choose wisely. Remember, you get to choose them before they choose you.

Chapter Four

How to Make Progress

*"Excellence is never an accident.
It is always the result of high intention, sincere effort,
and intelligent execution; it represents the wise choice
of many alternatives—choice, not chance,
determines your destiny."*

- Aristotle

Begin with the finish in mind

What do you want to do with your PhD? Think NOW before you begin! As a doctoral student you need to have a career plan in place at the start of your studies. If you enrol in a PhD for lack of better options or to delay entry into a poor job market, then you are likely to struggle with your PhD. This longer term end of the PhD process is covered in Chapter Five— Completing the PhD, Graduation and Beyond.

"He who has a WHY to live for can bear almost any HOW."

- Friedrich Nietzsche

Another more immediate end goal is a completed PhD thesis ready for submission. Borrow a PhD thesis and have a good look at it. You are going to have to write a thesis like this in order to get your PhD. Start working towards this goal from the very beginning of your PhD. It may seem like a distant or almost unachievable goal at the beginning (at least I felt that way), but you have to focus on the fact that you will write this document in order to get your PhD. An example of something to do right from the start is to keep good references, learn how to use referencing software such as Endnote, and use it as you go along. As part of your literature review, when you are reading a book, research paper etc. make good notes using your software. Don't do what I did! I read a number of very useful articles and books early on in my PhD but did not keep good references from what I was reading. In fact, I wrote notes in a number of booklets which were not correctly referenced and some of which were misplaced. Years later when writing up my thesis, I was not able to find the original book or article, and therefore, was not able to reference the material. It was frustrating but entirely my own fault. I should have started with the end in mind, knowing that I was going to need those references later. I did start to use free reference management software (called Mendeley) later on in my thesis writing, but I should have used this or other similar software right from the start.

Right from the beginning of your PhD always keep the end result in mind (completing your thesis) and everything you do should lead to achieving this result. Another important thing to do is to keep a research diary. In your diary write down all the details of your research as you go along. For example, if you are doing a survey, write down how you selected your survey sample. You may forget important details you need when writing up later (and it could be a number of years later). Write down everything you do and see and organise this material well. Write down your thoughts and reflections of what you are seeing and learning from your research. Your research diary will be invaluable when writing up your research later on.

> *"How we live our days, of course,
> is how we live our lives."*
> - Annie Dillard

Beware of the planning fallacy

The planning fallacy is a tendency for people and organisations to underestimate how long they will need to complete a task, even when they have experience of similar tasks over-running. The term was first proposed in a 1979 paper by Daniel Kahneman and Amos Tversky. When I began my PhD I had three years of funding and my plan was to complete in three years. I had heard that you can complete a PhD in three years and I assumed that I could do that, too. My own plan was anchored in what was the best case scenario as regards time to completion of a PhD. Actually, it took me six years to complete my PhD—double my internal forecast. The planning fallacy is when you are looking at your own case you construct a plan which is much more optimistic than a class of similar cases. If you want to know which view is more accurate, trust the outside view of average completion rates of PhDs and not your own internal view. We tend not to anticipate all the things that can happen to throw us off track. When planning, make as realistic an estimate as possible and then include a buffer—extra time and resources to cater for any unforeseen delays or cost overruns. In my own case I changed jobs, careers and continents, which had major implications for progress on my PhD. I had not anticipated any of these major events when I started. When planning, we tend to extrapolate from where we are into the future, but we cannot foresee events which will throw us off track.

In 2003, Lovallo and Kahneman proposed an expanded definition of the planning fallacy as the tendency to underestimate the time, costs, and risks of future actions and at the same time overestimate the benefits of the same. The latter has also proved true in my own case. I certainly overestimated the benefits of doing a PhD, and now two years post completion of my own PhD, I am certainly questioning its value. This is discussed further in Chapter Five.

Visualisation

Can you visualise your PhD completed? Can you visualise yourself confidently striding up to collect your degree certificate at your graduation ceremony? Can you see this vision? Engage all your five senses in the vision—see, hear, smell, taste and touch. Perhaps you have another vision of completing the PhD—

perhaps informing a loved one that you have finally finished and handed in your thesis and then embracing them? You need to make sure that whatever vision you have for completion of your PhD is programmed into your sub-conscious mind. Right now, I am visualising this book in print and there is no doubt about it—it will happen! I can feel the hardbound copy of the book in my hands and smell the smell of a newly printed book. Because you are reading this book, my vision has indeed come to pass. You need to do the same for your PhD thesis. Picture the finished hard bound copies of your thesis. Picture your graduation ceremony.

From my own personal experience I have found that the process of visualisation is very powerful and certainly helped me complete my PhD. I could see myself coming through the door carrying the hard bound copies of my thesis and excitedly showing my wife and children. I can still vividly see that image right now. In my mind's eye I could see my graduation ceremony and see my wife and children and other relatives seated at the ceremony. My children proudly watching their dad receive his PhD. I could hear the applause of the crowd for all the graduands. I could feel the embrace of my wife. Visualising this would make me literally cry. Emotion is the language of the subconscious mind. Using this process of visualisation you are setting an internal compass guiding you towards completion of your PhD.

"What we achieve inwardly will change outer reality."

- Plutarch, Greek Historian

My personal PhD vision was preceded by relaxation exercises, which make it easier for your vision to be embedded in your sub-conscious mind (this process is otherwise known as self-hypnosis). See the resources section at the end of this book for references to further information on visualisation. Relaxation helps change your brainwave activity from the normal awake state called Beta to the more relaxed Alpha state and more deeply relaxed Theta states. In a relaxed state your brain is more open to suggestion. You can write out a script of your vision of success—what you hear, see, smell, taste and feel. You can then record this vision on your computer or other digital device. You can then listen to your own recording over and over and visualise the associated mental pictures. Impress these images into your sub-conscious mind. Do you become emotional when you see these images in your mind? If so, then you are on the right track and are doing this correctly.

Many great sports people use this technique, which is called sports psychology in the world of sport. For example, world renowned boxer Muhammad Ali used to talk about creating his future history. In the days before a match, Muhammad would picture himself at the end of the fight with his arms lifted in the air and the referee proclaiming him the champion. He would visualise this very vividly and with total commitment and belief. He would hear the crowds cheering and shouting his name, he would feel how amazing it felt to be a winner. Tiger Woods, the famous golfer, apparently uses visualisation to concentrate on his game and visualise the perfect shot.

Through the process of visualisation you are also creating your future history—one where you have a PhD! There are also other benefits to learning self-hypnosis or visualisation. Dr John Arden, a California-based psychologist and neuropsychologist, wrote a book called *Rewire Your Brain*. The book is based on the recent developments in neuroscience and evidence-based treatment. At one point in the book Arden talks of the value of self-hypnosis, visualisation, meditation, sports physiology, prayer etc. in activating your para-sympathetic nervous system and helping you to relax. No matter what you call these practices, they have a similar effect on your brain. These practices are very good to bust stress and activate the frontal lobes of your brain, help you become more focussed and also promote neuroplasticity.

Reinforcing your PhD vision

While doing my PhD, in addition to visualisation, I also experimented with three other ways to constantly remind myself of the PhD goal which I wanted to achieve. I should have started doing this at the very beginning of my PhD, but I only started doing this in the later stages to try and propel myself forward and keep motivated and focussed on my PhD goal. You can certainly do all three of these practices at the same time. What you are seeking is to constantly remind yourself that your PhD goal is a priority and ensure that your sub-conscious mind is always taking you in the direction of your PhD goal.

1. Create a Vision Board

Cut out pictures from nice colour magazines and newspapers of things you want to achieve. You can also use your own photographs. The next step is to paste the images onto a large sheet of cardboard and then stick the sheet of cardboard with the images to the wall in your office/bedroom/study where you will see it constantly. The resulting collage of pictures will be a vision board; its purpose is to depict (and lead you to) your desired future. To remind myself of my PhD goal I pasted a picture onto my vision board of myself in academic dress, taken from an earlier graduation ceremony, with my new title—Dr.—in front of my name below the image. My goal of publishing a paper in a peer reviewed journal was also captured on my vision board. Once you make a vision board it just sits on your wall and is a constant reminder of your PhD related goal. I eventually achieved both of the PhD related goals on that vision board, so it worked for me. It can work for you, too.

2. Create a mind movie

A mind movie is a type of digital vision board which you can watch on your computer. I created one and then watched it every morning and evening. A mind movie is a short video clip of just a few minutes which features images related to all the goals you are trying to achieve, including your PhD. Motivational images related to your goals flash across your computer screen accompanied by background motivational music of your own choosing. I selected 'Eye of the Tiger' by the band, Survivor, as my background music. I used the same images of myself on my vision board in my mind movie. The result is that you are constantly reminding yourself of your PhD related goal. The addition of music which motivates you in your mind movie engages with your subconscious mind. You can use a website www.mindmovies.com or use video editing software on your computer to create your mind movie.

3. Write your PhD goal on a card and carry it with you

Write out your PhD related goal on a small business card and carry this card in your wallet or purse. Every time you open your wallet/purse you will see your PhD goal. Again, the purpose of this is to constantly remind yourself of your PhD related goal. At the moment I have a small card in my wallet with my key goals for the year written on the card. Every time I open my wallet I don't consciously see the card but I do find myself reviewing my key goals very often as a result of the card in my wallet. This tends to result in an impromptu review of progress towards achieving these goals which may only last a few moments. However, these impromptu reviews help to keep my goals at the forefront of my mind.

All of the above actions will help focus both your conscious and subconscious mind on your PhD goal. Harnessing the power of the sub-conscious mind is really important, as much of your thinking happens at the sub-conscious level. Once we align our conscious desire of completing the PhD with our sub-conscious thoughts then achieving our PhD goal will be much easier. Our subconscious mind is like an elephant, while our conscious mind is the rider on the elephant. What we want is the rider and elephant wanting to go in the same direction. If the elephant wants to go in a different direction to the rider then the elephant will always win. Hence, the importance of harnessing the power of your subconscious mind and getting your subconscious mind to take you in the direction of achieving your PhD. Self-hypnosis/visualisation, vision boards, mind movies and a reminder in your wallet or purse all help to impress your PhD goal on your sub-conscious mind.

Watch out for the rabbit trails

It took me much longer than it should have to complete my PhD and one reason was rabbit trails. While I should have been working on my PhD and getting the monkey off my back, I ended up doing some other things which distracted me from my goal. My advice is to get the monkey off your back (finish your

PhD) as soon as possible before it depresses you, drags you down or makes you bankrupt!

"Consider the postage stamp: its usefulness consists in the ability to stick to one thing till it gets there."

- Josh Billings, American Humourist

However, I engaged in other activities which distracted me from my PhD goal. I wrote and published a book on my subject area, which I should not have done at the time. I should have focussed on finishing my PhD. I also completed a one year course and passed an exam in hypnotherapy, including working with clients to lose weight and quit smoking while I was doing my PhD. Hypnotherapy was completely unrelated to the subject of my PhD, and again, was a distraction and a delay to getting my PhD finished (although it did teach me to visualise my PhD goal, which was very useful). I should, however, have focussed 100% of my efforts on my PhD and on getting it done. My advice is to stick to the plan and don't allow diversions (rabbit trails). In the latter years of my PhD I also wrote and published a research paper related to my PhD in a peer reviewed journal, but that did actually help me complete my PhD, and therefore, was not a diversion.

Quit or never quit?

According to Lovitts (2001) graduate schools have faced attrition (quit) rates of approximately 50 percent for the past 40 years, so the issue of whether to quit or not is a really important issue. There is one school of thought that says take a break if you must, but never quit. You may have heard the saying that "quitters never win."

> *"It's not that I'm so smart; it's just that I stay with problems longer."*
>
> - Albert Einstein

You must persist with your goal no matter what. No matter what happens you must be resilient and keep going. Yes, these characteristics will probably get you your PhD. Right now I am reasonably OKAY with the fact that I did not quit my PhD, but is it always the right decision not to quit? Perhaps in my own case I lacked the courage to quit (it does take a lot of courage). I was afraid to disappoint my supervisor and the organisation which provided my financial support. Would they demand their money back? I was not even sure how I would feel about myself (would I feel like a loser?). I did not have the courage to walk away from my PhD, and in essence, I was trapped in a prison of my own making. If you keep hanging in there you will hopefully reach the end of the PhD journey and eventually graduate as I did. One downside of quitting is that it may shake your confidence to achieve tough goals. If you quit the PhD will you trust yourself again to start and complete a long and arduous goal? When you have completed the PhD, toughed it out, then hopefully, you will have a shot of confidence—I can do anything now!

Another way to look at this is that if you realise that the PhD is not for you halfway through your studies then perhaps it is best to leave the PhD and pivot to something more in line with what you really want. Perhaps the assumptions you made about doing a PhD were wrong, your circumstances have changed during the PhD or you realise the associated costs of doing a PhD are just too high. You may not also be able to see any career progression using the PhD or have become bored with your topic and want to move your life in a different direction. Stephen R. Covey, American author of the book, *7 Habits of Highly Effective People*, talks of it this way: "If the ladder is not leaning against the right wall, every step we take just gets us to the wrong place faster..."

You must face the brutal facts that you are on the wrong path—this is hard, and takes a lot of courage. The concept of pivoting is from the business world and made popular by Eric Reis in his book, *The Lean Startup*. In the business world, pivoting is rarely the same as "quitting"—it means a correction in course, changing things to find a more profitable enterprise. The decision to stay the course or leave the PhD and pivot to something new is for you alone. This is your life and your time. Life is not a dress rehearsal; you only get one shot at it (as far as we know!).

An issue to be aware of in your decision to continue or to quit is the *sunk cost effect,* which is the tendency for humans to continue investing in something that clearly isn't working/is wrong for them. A sunk cost is money and/or time that has already been spent and cannot be recovered. Sunk costs are also called retrospective costs. Logic dictates that because sunk costs will not change—no matter what actions are taken—they should not play a role in decision-making. Emotionally, however, the more someone invests time, effort and money on something, the harder it becomes to leave it and move on. You continue investing your time and energy into your PhD because you have already invested so much in it, and therefore, how could you possibly walk away? You must realise however, that if you know for sure that this is wrong for you for whatever reason that the time and money invested already are not recoverable. You need to be able to walk away; continuing on the same path and investing further time and money in something that is wrong for you does not make sense.

Philip McKernan, an Irish motivational speaker living in Canada, debates the issue of moving on/letting go in an online video. Philip advises that if you know something is not serving you—let go. If you know this in your heart and soul—let go. That is not quitting. However, if what you are pursuing (in this case your PhD or the career opportunities it will bring you) is truly your dream, then stay the course. See the Philip's video at the following web address: http://philipmckernan.com/letting-go-or-quitting/.

The effects of doctoral attrition

Student attrition is the reduction in numbers of students attending courses as time goes by (students who leave the course for whatever reason). Golde (2000) talks of the high rates of student attrition (40-50%) and students 'leaving quietly' and the issue not being given much attention. I had not reflected on the possible consequences of dropping out of my PhD before I researched the topic for this book. There appears to be two broad ways individuals can see dropping out—as a broadly positive experience, which McKernan describes above as 'letting go,' and a more negative giving up, although you would actually prefer to continue. Barbara E. Lovitts (Lovitts, 2001) published a book titled *Leaving the Ivory Tower: The Causes and Consequences of Departure from Doctoral Study*. In the book, Lovitts makes the point that student attrition is commonly thought to be the fault of the student who is 'under-qualified, disinterested or unfocused.' As a result students can feel responsible for their own failure. Students' personal lives may be devastated as they spend years explaining why they did not finish the degree (Sternberg, 1981). The emotional impact of attrition causes some to struggle with bouts of serious depression and has even resulted in a few cases of violence and attempted suicide (Hinchey & Kimmel, 2000; Lovitts, 2001). Lovitts conducted a study that included surveys of non-completers and concluded that attrition is largely due to a breakdown in the 'academic integration' that needs to occur to support doctoral students to completion.

Academic integration includes having enough information about program requirements and department processes as well as socio-emotional support systems involving faculty and other students. Lovitts places strong emphasis on the strength of the student-supervisor relationship. Other reasons for student attrition include inadequate funding, procrastination, incongruence between student goals and program focus and low researcher self-efficacy. Self-efficacy is the extent or strength of one's belief in one's own ability to complete tasks and reach goals.

Another issue which may impact on student attrition is the choice of academic discipline. According to Tamburri (2013), a 2006 study prepared for the Social Sciences and Humanities Research Council showed that students in the humanities and social sciences take about a year longer to complete their degrees and are more likely to abandon their studies than their colleagues in sciences and engineering. Students in the humanities and social sciences are more likely to devote several years working towards a degree before abandoning it. Students in the social sciences and humanities more often work alone, while those in the natural and health sciences collaborate on research projects with colleagues and supervisors. Research shows that students who work in teams are less likely to abandon their studies. In another a study by Willis and Carmichael (2011), six late-stage doctoral non completers from counsellor education programs participated in research interviews. Out of the six, five participants reported a negative experience of leaving their PhD, and one student reported a positive experience of leaving. Students who had a negative experience reported shame and embarrassment of letting a former mentor down. Some participants reported that the emotional consequences were felt for an extended period of time. It took considerable time for some candidates to admit to themselves and others that they were not going to get their PhD. Another candidate suffered from regret about what could have been had they continued their PhD. Another candidate suffered from depression after leaving the PhD, which also had a negative impact on his relationship with his wife. It is interesting to note that the study participants who had a negative reaction to leaving their PhD all described how a problematic relationship with their dissertation chair (supervisor) played a significant role in their attrition.

In the Willis and Carmichael study, the student who reported a positive experience of leaving the PhD had progressed to a late stage in the PhD but no longer wanted to continue because of a reassessment of personal goals. The candidate decided to leave on her own after she realised that she began doctoral study in part to prove to her father that she was capable of doing it. She had endured his criticisms as a child and had set out on a path to prove to him once and for all that she was a smart and capable woman. She realised that this was a poor motivation to be doing a PhD and that she had nothing to prove to her father. For this woman leaving her PhD programme resulted in positive emotional reactions, such as relief and peace. She felt happy about her decision to leave her PhD and she now had free time and money again, which was a relief. She no longer wanted the degree and thus, experienced positive emotions related to attrition. This is akin to what McKernan describes as 'letting go,' so it's a positive decision to move on from the PhD.

My own PhD was in the social sciences, and I worked alone with little interaction with other students for years. I can see now that my desire to abandon my PhD even up to quite late in the process was not that unexpected. I can also see that the good relationship and support I received from my academic supervisor was instrumental in my completion of the PhD. I can understand all this now, retrospectively, but at the time I had not read about the causes of doctoral student attrition. I was too busy working on my dissertation to understand the wider issues of what I was experiencing.

In summary, if you do want to quit your PhD make sure that you are quitting because you want to let go or pivot to something better and not because you have problems such as a poor relationship with your supervisor and a general lack of support from your university. If your reasons to quit relate to 'academic integration' issues, and you really don't want to quit, then make sure and tackle these problems by discussing them with your supervisor and academic institution. If you drop out when you don't really want to then this can result in a negative emotional reaction as discussed above.

Golde (2000), in a paper titled 'Should I stay or should I go?' Student descriptions of the doctoral attrition process,' presents three detailed case studies of students who left their PhD programme. It is well worth reading these cases to get a better understanding of student attrition from the student's perspective.

Focus on the NOW

> *"Do not spend any time in day dreaming or castle building; hold to the one vision of what you want, and act now."*
>
> — Wallace D. Wattles

The only time we really have to do anything is in the present moment, or the *Now*. Think about it. We only have control over the present moment. We cannot change the moment that has passed, nor can we act in the future. As we live, we seem to move through a succession of *Nows*. To succeed in doing a PhD—or anything else for that matter—we have to pull ourselves into the present moment and stop being distracted by random useless thought. That is where learning to focus on the present moment is really important. The present moment, the Now, is where you conduct your research and write your PhD thesis. Frequently in my own case I was paralysed from taking action in the Now by useless thoughts like:

- Why am I doing this PhD?
- Is it really necessary?
- Am I smart enough to get a PhD?

- Am I good enough?
- I don't feel like it now but I will start on the PhD tomorrow.

The end result of these thoughts was that I was squandering the only time I had to do anything and make progress on my PhD—I was squandering the Now. Well, tomorrow does not come—all we have is the present moment—so act Now. Do something, do anything, but act. It is amazing that once you do begin to act in the Now that you build momentum, and you may find that once you start then you do not want to stop! Pull yourself into the present moment and act! Another important point is that doing it Now is more important than doing it right. Do not worry if you feel what are doing is not good enough. Take action—whatever it is—Now. The more you can take action, the faster you can get your PhD done. We do live in an age of distraction—email, the internet, smartphones, text messages, apps, TV, Facebook etc. all potential distractions. We need to be able to switch off these distractions. Cancel email alters, mute the phone and put it away. A useful acronym to pull your attention into the now and prioritise your attention is W.I.N., which stands for 'What's Important Now.' Put this acronym somewhere you can see it so that it will remind you to pull yourself back to the present and help you to focus on the most important thing you should be doing at this moment (which may be working on your PhD or may be spending quality time with your partner etc.).

"To go far you must begin near and the nearest step is the most important one."

- Jiddu Krishnamurti, Indian Philosopher

The PhD is an Iterative Process

The most likely way you can fail to make progress on your PhD is if you give up and stop working on it. As discussed earlier, however, if you decide the PhD is not for you, and you decide to let go and do something different, that is not failure, but it takes courage to walk away.

Doing a PhD is an iterative process. Iteration means the act of repeating a process with the aim of approaching a desired goal, target or result. Each repetition of the process is also called an iteration, and the results of one iteration are used as the starting point for the next iteration. Each iteration brings you closer to the desired outcome. You just keep refining and improving whatever you are working on until it gets done. It is part of the PhD process to make mistakes, learn, change and try again—over and over.

PhD by Kaizen

Kaizen is the Japanese process for gradual improvement. Small actions compounded over time reveal considerable results, either positive or negative. A myriad of small actions compounded over time will get you your PhD, starting with the next small action which is in front of you right now. That is it! There are no quick fix solutions—it's a slow process—but keep chipping away at it every day and you will make progress and eventually complete. What slows you will be to stop and take a break for too long. Then it is hard to re-start. Make a habit of making progress daily and build momentum. What you must do right now is focus on the next task at hand.

I love the title of the book, *Writing your Dissertation in 15 minutes a Day*, by Joan Bolker. The title says it all. What it conveys is the concept of 'Kaizen' discussed above—make at least a little bit of progress every day on your PhD and you will get there in the end. When you pick up a completed thesis or research paper, what you don't see is all the refining and re-writing and the different iterations which contributed to that finished product. What you also don't see is someone taking small daily actions on their PhD, such as writing each word, line and each paragraph, one by one, day by day, which builds up to the final product.

All difficult things have their origin in that which is easy, and great things in that which is small.

- Lao-Tzu

Work with your supervisor

In order to make progress on your PhD it is important to meet your supervisor regularly and set work targets between meetings. One of my own failings was being afraid to share my work with my supervisor in case he felt it was too poor. When you get to the point of having done your best at something let it go and share it. You must share drafts of your work to get feedback and move on to the next and improved version of your work. You need to get feedback to move to the next level. You will have hundreds of revisions and refinements along the way. Assuming that you have shared your work you also must take feedback well from your supervisor. Your supervisor should know very well what a PhD requires and what needs to be done.

There is no point being excessively defensive about your work. Good feedback from your supervisor will start with the positive mention in clear and specific terms of what aspects need improvement and how to achieve them, and end with the positive. Constructive feedback is important as it contributes to a positive atmosphere, nurturing self-confidence and self-esteem in the receiver. By feedback being concrete and specific, it prevents misunderstandings and reduces the likelihood of negative feelings, uncertainty and resentment. Unfortunately, not all supervisors may be as constructive and specific as they should be in their feedback, but this is what should happen.

Time management

The PhD project is just like any other project which requires you to come up with a strategy on how you are going to manage your time. Myers (1999) found that poor time management is a factor in doctoral degree non-completion. Time management is the process of planning and deciding the amount of time spent on specific activities. Once you develop some good time management habits you will automatically make progress on your PhD. In my experience a key aspect of time management is to get a routine going—to develop positive habits which will propel you to success.

"Ill Habits Gather by Unseen Degrees;
As brooks make rivers, rivers run to seas."

- Ovid

The power of habit

"All our life.... is but a mass of habits--practical, emotional, and intellectual--systematically organized, for our weal or woe, and bearing us irresistibly toward our destiny, whatever the latter may be."

- William James, American philosopher and psychologist

Failure is not a single, disastrous occasion. You don't fail overnight. Instead, failure is a few errors in judgement, repeated every day. The corollary to this is that success is a few positive steps repeated daily. For myself, I discovered after struggling to make progress on my PhD for a number of years that I am a morning person. When are you most productive? Make use of that time for your PhD. My strategy was to get up at 5:00 a.m. each morning and work on my PhD. I would get up at least six days a week at 5:00 a.m. Before I came up with this strategy I did not make much progress on my PhD. After getting up at 5:00 a.m. and having a cup of coffee, I would meditate for 10 minutes in order to focus my mind (see the resources section at the end of the book for resources on meditation). I also created a mind movie of my goals, as mentioned earlier. This is a series of photographs linked to my goals with a background sound track—'Eye of the Tiger' by the band, Survivor. I would watch my mind movie on my laptop, which would focus my mind on the end result I was after—to complete my PhD and my other goals. After meditating and watching my mind movie I would start straight away working on my PhD. I followed the philosophy of eating a frog for breakfast as outlined in the book written by Brian Tracey—(*Eat That Frog! 21 Great Ways to Stop Procrastinating and Get More Done in Less Time*). The concept is to do the thing you most dislike doing the first thing in the morning. In my experience it is sometimes very difficult to face into writing the PhD, especially when you have to start a new chapter or to work on something you don't like (for me, statistics!). However, I found that if I started straight away in the morning then I would build up momentum quickly and by breakfast time I would have already two hours' work completed on my PhD (from 5.30 a.m. to 7.30 a.m.). This was a great feeling each morning to have had two hours' work under your belt when sitting down for breakfast! I would find that later on in the day I would have an unstoppable momentum to make progress and I would feel really positive and happy!

However, if I was to get up late and start into the PhD about 9:00 a.m., I would find it almost impossible to get started and end up procrastinating. One of my biggest ways to procrastinate was to plan endlessly. Since I completed my PhD I have continued with my habit of starting early and eating the frog for breakfast. I have written this book by spending only 30 minutes every morning writing (from 5.30 a.m. to 6:00 a.m.) and then heading off to work. That is only half an hour per day, but over time the results build up and eventually you end up with a completed book! It's a good idea to understand how habits work. A book by Charles Duhigg, *The Power of Habit*, describes the habit loop, whereby an environmental cue automatically leads to a behavioural routine which results in a reward. Once a habit becomes established it becomes effortless. I did mention above that I started the habit of getting up at 5:00 a.m., which is one of my really important productivity habits. I really struggled to get up early in the beginning. However, I notice now that the habit is so firmly embedded in my brain that I find it very difficult to lie in bed beyond 5:00 a.m.! The cue is my alarm going off where I jump from bed and go downstairs to the kitchen (action) and have my only cup of coffee of the day (reward). This routine happens with no conscious effort from me. It usually takes me about half an hour to fully wake up, but it doesn't matter, as I am on autopilot.

Another key habit I developed was doing a daily review and planning session for the following day. I also developed the habit of doing a weekly review and planning session each week. During your review sessions reflect on what is working or not working and make small changes. If you planned to work on your PhD today and things did not go according to plan, reflect on that. Reflect on why things did not work and how you can improve for tomorrow. Adjust your plan. Make a habit of continuous slow improvement.

Another key habit was going to bed early; by 9:00 p.m. to 9.30 p.m. I am in bed relaxing and reading a book. At the same time I jettisoned some bad habits, such as staying up late mindlessly watching TV. Another key habit I developed was keeping fit and healthy—a healthy diet and regular exercise is really important. Get out and get fresh air and clear your head. Build exercise into your routine and make it a habit. Regular exercise and a healthy diet will lift your mood and keep you energised as you work on your PhD. A daily prayer for support from above will also not be uncalled for.

Use of a smartphone app to monitor and track habits is useful. You can search for and try different apps and choose the one which suits you best. One particular smartphone app which I use is called the Habit Factor. There is also a useful book for sale (Grunburg, 2010) and video to watch on the related website. See the Useful Online Resources at the back of this book for further details.

Examine your own habits to understand what triggers certain habitual behaviour. Consciously build habits which will propel you to complete your PhD.

"Routine, in an intelligent man, is a sign of ambition."

- W. H. Auden

Chunk down your work

How do you eat an elephant? The answer, of course, is one bite at a time. In other words, you can only do one small piece of work on your PhD at a time. Therefore, break your work down into pieces and set sub-goals and associated tasks.

"It is not enough to take steps which may someday lead to a goal; each step must be itself a goal and a step likewise."

- Johann Wolfgang von Goethe

In discussions with your PhD supervisor agree what you need to do by the next time you meet. Your PhD will be made up of multiple small goals and associated tasks over a number of years. As mentioned already one of my favourite ways to procrastinate from working on my PhD was to keep planning and not actually work on my PhD. I tried many methods of planning out my work, including different software programmes. Eventually, I found a good computer software programme to break down my PhD goals and tasks into manageable chunks. The software is called Goalenforcer Hyperfocus, and it is very visual, intuitive and easy to use (see the References and Useful Resources section towards the end of this book on 'Useful computer software' for further details). In the screen shot below taken from my own PhD action plan you can see goals and tasks broken down into subcomponents. It is very easy to drag and drop these tasks, and each is given a start date and finish date. You can turn any task into a sub-goal by adding one or more subtasks to it and break down your work into easy bite-sized chunks. Tasks are colour coded automatically by the software. Current tasks are orange, completed tasks are green and overdue tasks are red.

Aim to meet deadlines agreed with your supervisor, and you can use this software to track progress. These interim deadlines will propel you forward. The text in the top left hand corner of the screenshot in Figure 1 below tells you where you are in relation to the overall goal at the top and all the sub-goals in between. Once you complete all the tasks related to a goal then the goal is ticked off. Eventually, all the goals, sub-goals and tasks will be done and you will be finished your PhD! The software is so simple and easy to use that within a short time you can develop a plan of what you need to do and which small piece to work on in the *Now*. In fact, having completed my PhD, I still use this software to plan out all my goals, which shows how useful and easy to use this software is.

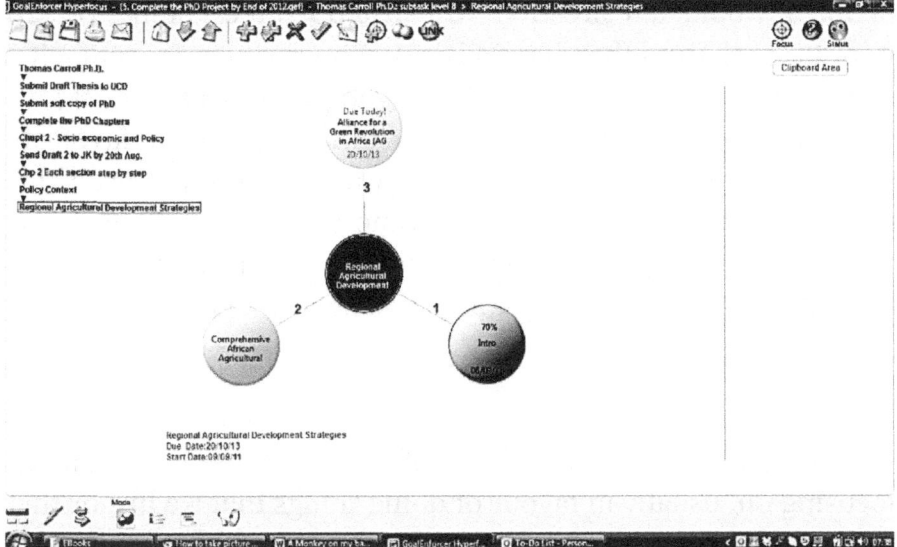

Figure 1: Screenshot of 'GoalEnforcer Hyperfocus' software which I used to plan out my PhD sub-goals and tasks.

Chunk down your time

You can also break down your time into chunks and focus on doing one chunk of PhD related work at a time. What you focus on during each chunk will be determined by what sub-goals and tasks you are working on (as determined by your plan). During a chunk I did not allow myself to do anything else except the PhD. No internet surfing, Facebook, emails etc.! Initially, I used a clock to measure a chunk of time, such as 20 minutes. I later used an app called Pomodoroido on my smart phone to measure each chunk. You can also buy a Pomodoro timer (see http://pomodorotechnique.com/).

I chunked down my time when I was finding it particularly hard to focus and get things done. I might give myself a break for a few minutes between chunks to surf the internet as a reward for completing a chunk. Or I might do three chunks and then take a break. I would tell myself I will just do three chunks (of 20 minutes each) and then have a break. You can also set yourself a daily target of chunks to do. When you hit your daily goal give yourself a reward. Perhaps some TV time and watch a favourite show etc.—something that will motivate you today. I used this technique of spending chunks of time on my PhD when I was really finding the going tough and finding it hard to push myself to make progress. It is simple and it really worked for me.

Dealing with procrastination

Procrastination is when we put off tasks which we should be focusing on, usually in favour of doing things that we like or that make us feel comfortable. We do more pleasurable tasks in place of less pleasurable ones, and thus putting off looming tasks to a later time. I found that procrastination was a major issue for me and was a big factor in my taking twice as long as planned to complete my PhD. Procrastination may also be an obstacle to you achieving your PhD related goals. The first step to dealing with procrastination is to recognise that you are doing it. Prioritise tasks which you have to do, and if you are not tackling your top priority tasks then you need to take action. Another sign of procrastination is to acknowledge tasks which need to be done and not starting them. Once you recognise that you are procrastinating the second step is to understand why you are doing it. Either you find the task unpleasant or you find the task overwhelming. Once you have identified why you are procrastinating then you can move on to the third step, which is tackling the problem.

A. If you find a task unpleasant:

- Promise yourself a reward when you complete the task. The reward does not have to be huge. In my own case I used to promise myself some time to surf the internet when I completed a particular task. Or I might say to myself that I cannot take a break until the task is completed.

- Make a commitment to someone that you will do the task and ask them to hold you accountable. This creates a social pressure to complete the task.

- Focus on the unpleasant consequences of not getting the task done. This will have the effect of bringing the future negative consequence of not doing the task into the present moment and motivate you to act now. It's easier to procrastinate when the unpleasant consequences of not doing something seem far off.

B. If you are overwhelmed:

- Break the project down into more manageable tasks (chunk it down).

- Then start with the easy ones, even if these are not the most logical first actions. This will give you momentum and make the whole project less daunting.

As mentioned earlier, eating the frog first thing in the morning (doing an unpleasant task) was a great way for me to beat procrastination and make progress on my PhD. However, you can also tackle the easy actions as a way to get started and get momentum. Chunking it down was also a great way for me to beat procrastination using the GoalEnforcer software, which I also found fun to use. Having a clear vision in your mind of what you are aiming for, as discussed earlier in this chapter, is also very important to beat procrastination. Much of our lives are controlled by our sub-conscious thoughts. Once you have the goal of a completed PhD firmly embedded in your sub-conscious mind this will inevitably propel your towards your goal.

Don't be alone

Doing a PhD can be a very lonely journey. When I was an undergraduate I had a large class of fellow students to share my frustrations and challenges with as well as my celebrations. The same applied when I completed my master's degree. The class size was smaller for the master's degree, but I still had fellow students to share with and to turn to when support was needed. However, when I was doing my PhD I was very much alone (class size of one!). It was just me working on my own research and occasionally checking in with my supervisor. When I began my PhD I was on a different continent to my supervisor and the university, so it was particularly difficult for me. I felt isolated from the university and did not really understand what was expected from me. I had no contact with any other PhD student, so I did not have anyone to turn to who was on the same path as me. I did, of course, have my immediate family for support, which was really important and kept me going. Are your family and friends supportive? You need this support from your loved ones to keep you going when things become difficult.

In addition to the support of immediate family and friends I would recommend that you find out who is starting a PhD in your faculty around the same time as you, get their contacts and get to know them. Keep in touch and meet up every so often and share frustrations and tips on how to make progress. Perhaps your university already organises this type of networking amongst PhD students, but if not, I recommend doing it anyway. At the end of the day nobody can understand what you are going through better than someone who is going through the same process as yourself. It is very reassuring when you hear from other PhD students how they are struggling with their PhD the same as you.

There are no straight lines

When you see a beautifully bound completed thesis you may think that the person who wrote it clearly knew what they were doing at all times and everything went smoothly from beginning to end. You do not see all the struggles, the confusion at times, the changes of direction and jumping back and forth between stages of the PhD which went to make this document. You don't see the times of rapid progress on the PhD, times of no progress at all and times of slow, plodding progress. Reading the thesis it may appear that the PhD process is linear from beginning to end. You come up with your original research idea, conduct your research, do your analysis and write up the finished thesis. In reality you will be jumping back and forth between stages. For example, you may be at the writing up stage of your PhD but still be going back to review references or going back to analyse the data again because a new idea came up on what analysis to undertake. I had to go back to data collection when doing my analysis to fill a gap in my data. My literature review was not done in one neat block; it was worked on at different stages of the thesis. For some of my chapters I wrote about six different drafts before I reached the final version.

The important thing to remember is that when you are faced with a blank screen, just type. Get your ideas out of your head and into your computer. Do the best you can but do not be overly concerned about quality at this stage. You do not have to do perfect work. You will then have a first draft of your results or of a chapter. Draft one can be shared and feedback received. This is the basis of draft two etc. A thesis is going to evolve over multiple revisions. You will further clarify and refine what you write, fill gaps and add additional material and sections. You will add additional references. You will continue refining drafts of your work in response to feedback until both you and your supervisor are happy.

In the beginning I had a block about releasing my draft work to my supervisor. This was because subconsciously, I was afraid that he would think my work was below the standard required. My subconscious thinking was an impediment to my progress, because without his feedback on the work I could not move to produce a better version of my work. It is important that you realise that it's okay to produce drafts of your work which you are not fully happy with and to release your work for constructive criticism. Your supervisor cannot do his or her job without material to critique, so make sure to deliver drafts of your work at the agreed time. Remember the saying, "Doing it now is more important than doing it right." Focus on completing drafts of your work—there will be plenty of time later for further refinements and working on improving the quality with each iteration.

Chronology of my PhD

As discussed in the last section, your work on the PhD will not go in straight lines. As the old military saying goes, plans are good until you come in contact with the enemy. You may have the best laid plans and intentions at the start of your PhD on how you will finish within a certain timeframe—all very neat and linear. However, you must expect things to work out differently as life gets in the way of your best laid plans.

> *"Life is what happens to you while you're busy making other plans."*
>
> - Allen Saunders American writer, journalist and cartoonist

A number of unforeseen things happened during the course of my PhD. I moved country and continent as I moved with my family from Kenya to live in Ireland. This change was precipitated by family issues which required me to move back to Ireland. We also experienced the 2007 and 2008 post-election violence in Kenya, which made us seriously question our future in the country. Leaving Kenya was a major change for both my family and I. Although I am originally Irish, I had lived in Kenya for 15 years and returning home was a major reverse culture shock. It was equally very difficult for my wife, who was born and lived all her life in Kenya, and my children, who were also born and raised in Kenya. I also had to choose where to live in Ireland, find accommodation and find a new job. During this major change I had to remember that I was also doing a PhD. To be frank, I made little or no progress on my PhD for about a year.

During the course of my PhD I also changed jobs three times. Each of these jobs was very different with different challenges and responsibilities. When I started my PhD I was working with an agricultural college in Kenya as a project manager. When I returned to Ireland the first job I worked at was with an international charity dealing with development programmes in Africa. The second job was working with a small hypnotherapy practice supporting clients to solve personal problems such as quit smoking, lose weight and combat depression. The third job was as a university lecturer coordinating a programme in rural development and supporting students obtaining their degrees. I had not foreseen these changes, but all the while I had to continue working on my PhD in the background.

When I returned to Ireland I also bought a house and obtained a mortgage, which involved a move from the house I had rented when I returned from Africa. I also raised a family and generally had to do all that I was doing as I wrote the PhD!

During this time I was also involved in two court cases relating to property. One was in Kenya where we had purchased property, and the vendor, after receiving payment, refused to transfer the property. Due to the slowness of the Kenyan judicial system the case is still not completed ten years later! The other case was in Ireland and involved family conflict over land. The later was particularly difficult. All the while, however, the PhD still had to be done! It was always there in the background.

You will have ups and downs; sometimes you will make little progress and sometimes you will get a wind at your back and make great progress. Some days other life events will be more distracting and may throw you off course. Accept that you may be thrown off course by life events at times, but as long as you get back to working on your PhD you will eventually achieve your goal. I got a particular positive break when I got a temporary six month contract with the university where I was also registered as a PhD student. Being on the staff and dealing with student theses helped me and gave me the motivation to write and progress my own thesis. My PhD supervisor also became my boss, which also helped as I was in close contact with him and my PhD was always on my mind. This position gave me the final push to complete my PhD.

Much of the time during my PhD I was off course, behind and frustrated—not getting stuff finished on time, missing deadlines and missing work submission dates. But in the end I still got to my final destination and completed my PhD. If you are in the position of being always behind and late—okay, it's not the best but it certainly does not mean you will fail. In the end you will succeed as long as you do not give up. An often repeated analogy is a plane headed to a particular destination. The plane is off course for most of the journey but it continually adjusts its course and gets back on the right path. Winds then push it off course again. It adjusts again to compensate for the winds. This happens continuously throughout the journey. The plane eventually gets to the final destination in the end! You will be blown off course during your PhD, but as long as you keep your final destination in mind and keep readjusting your path to the PhD to get yourself back on track, you will reach your final destination in the end.

Working and doing a PhD

I have a wife and three children to support and I had to work during my PhD to support my family. Working fulltime and doing a PhD at the same time is particularly hard. You have all the demands of work and at the same time have to juggle the time needed to input into the PhD. You need to keep momentum with your PhD as you also work. While I was working in Kenya this was easy as my work and PhD overlapped. The two were closely intertwined. My PhD was also part of my work which allowed me to collect my data. However, when I returned to Ireland my PhD was no longer directly related to my work. I had to work a full day and then try and squeeze in the PhD and my family time. I was commuting to work by train, and my train ride was about one hour to and from work each day. During the commute time, especially in the mornings, I would try to work on my laptop for perhaps 50 minutes or so. It was an early morning train and while everyone else was snoozing I was working on my PhD! Many weekends were also devoted to the PhD. There was not much time left for family. Sometimes I would go off track when work was busy or I had work trips abroad. I would leave the PhD for long periods of time without doing anything. I would then have to get myself back into the PhD and try and pick up where I left off the last time. I would also have to struggle with all my accompanying negative thoughts such as 'Why am I doing this?' 'This is too hard.' 'I am not smart enough.' 'I will never finish,' etc. Stopping and starting is not advisable—aim to keep the momentum going and keep working continuously on your PhD even if you can only afford a small amount of time each day to work on it.

After two years, I left the job which involved commuting and I was working from home and my wife was working fulltime. Now I had greater control over my schedule and was able to make much faster progress on my PhD. I was able to work five hours or more on my PhD per day and spend time with my family. Towards the end of my PhD when I worked at the university I made good progress on my PhD as I was now in an academic environment and my work overlapped with my PhD again.

Overall, during the course of my PhD there were times when I was in the doldrums and making little or no progress and then there were times of more rapid progress. The key lesson I learned was always aim to make at least some progress on a daily basis. Even if you only have a small period of time and are very busy—keep the momentum going. This will carry you through the tough times and into times when you can make more rapid progress.

How to manage stress

Exercise is a key way to combat stress. Make sure to build some exercise into your daily routine. You may play a sport—great. If you are not sporty then you can aim to go for a walk every day or at least three or four times per week. Aim to build exercise into your routine so that it becomes habitual for you to exercise. You should also maintain a good healthy diet of a wide variety of healthy fruits, vegetables, grains and sources of protein. Avoid excessive consumption of caffeine and alcohol. I limited the consumption of coffee to one cup per day first thing in the morning (my reward for an early rise). Excessive consumption of alcohol can interfere with your work. The day following consumption of alcohol you will likely feel drowsy and hung over, which will negatively impact progress on your PhD. If you do like a drink then perhaps a nice bottle of wine or your favourite tipple with friends or partner can be a reward for achieving a PhD related goal. For example, you may have been working on a draft chapter for a number of weeks and have just submitted it to your supervisor.

Learning how to control negative thoughts is also a way to control stress. In many cases it is not events themselves which are stressful but our negative thoughts about them which we keep going over and over in our minds. Learn to step back, take a breather and analyse the situation.

When our 'inner critic' or self-talk tells us we are stupid or going to fail etc.—tell it to shut up!

Learn how to meditate. Meditation is a great way to de-stress. Learn how to switch off and relax your body and mind. Learn how to be in the present moment. Build meditation into your daily routine. I meditate every day at the start of my day, and I do find that there are positive benefits such as being able to de-stress and being more focussed at work. Please see the resources section at the end of the book for further resources on meditation.

Perhaps you have a hobby, enjoy working with your hands or playing a musical instrument. These activities can also help you unwind and give you something to look forward to at the end of your working day. When you achieve you PhD related goal for the day or particular quota of work that you set for yourself you can reward yourself with some enjoyable time spent on your hobby.

Also make time for your friends and family. Life still has to go on during your PhD. Aim to make some time where you can switch off, relax and do something fun with your friends or family. If you have a good routine and have your quota of work done for the day or the week or have achieved whatever mini goal you set yourself on your PhD then you will feel you deserve your time off. If you have not done what you planned on your PhD then you will likely feel guilty even if you take some time off. Make sure you earn your time off and you will enjoy your time off much more.

Another way to reduce stress is to have good plans in place and know you are making steady progress on your PhD. Even if you feel that you are not sure what you are doing, where you are on your PhD journey or what a PhD is. Do not worry, I have been there in your shoes and still went on to complete my PhD. There are times for everything during your PhD journey. There are times for confusion and times for clarity. Keep working at the PhD day by day, bit by bit and things will become clear. A fellow PhD candidate once described doing a PhD to me as being analogous with churning butter out of milk. Initially, you will slosh the milk around and nothing will happen. Eventually, however, if you keep sloshing the milk around, butter will form out of the milk as a result of all your efforts. A PhD is like this; you will stumble around initially, perhaps feeling like you are not making much progress, but eventually your PhD will take shape from all your efforts. Once you are achieving your mini goals and making daily progress on your PhD this is a good feeling.

Stopping work on your PhD for long periods is depressing and stressful. The PhD is hanging over you and you are not making any progress. If you find yourself in this situation act today, do something, anything to get yourself re-started on your PhD. Once you re-start, even in a small way, you will pick up momentum. Remember Newton's Law of motion—a body in rest tends to stay at rest, and a body in motion tends to stay in motion. Make sure you keep your momentum on the PhD; it's much easier to keep up this momentum than if you stop working at your PhD and then have to restart.

A final point here on how to manage stress is to turn to others for help if your PhD is stressing you. Share your problem with your family, friends, fellow PhD students or PhD supervisor.

Have a frank discussion—don't assume they know what is going on. Remember the old expression—a problem shared is a problem halved.

For those who would like to read further on this important issue see a book listed in the reference section by Kadison, R., & Foy DiGeronimo, T. (2004) titled *College of the Overwhelmed: The Campus Mental Health Crisis and What to Do About It*. The UK's Guardian newspaper published a series of articles in 2014 titled 'Mental health: a university crisis.' To read this series: http://www.theguardian.com/education/series/mental-health -a-university-crisis.

Chapter Four summary

It is important to begin your PhD firmly focussed on the end you seek—begin with the end in mind. You are aiming to submit your thesis and fulfil all the requirements of the institution where you are registered. Know what is expected of you and aim to achieve this right from the very beginning. You can use visualisation as a way to embed the image of your final destination (completed PhD) in your subconscious mind. This is a powerful way to set yourself up for success. There are always going to be distractions along the way to getting your PhD. Stay focussed and aim to get your PhD finished as soon as possible. If you find along the way that a PhD is not for you and you wish to quit, it takes real courage to walk away. In the end only you can make this decision for what is best for you.

Along the way to your PhD stay focussed, stay present. Now is the only time you have so focus on what you need to do today. The only time you have to work on your PhD is the present moment and to make progress you must avoid distracting and useless thoughts and simply take action. It's all about persistence and making progress. Consistent daily action will carry you to successfully completing your PhD. Set numerous mini goals along the way with your supervisor and do not be afraid to share early drafts. A PhD is an iterative process and each successive draft will be better. Build a daily work routine that works for you. Break down your work into bite-sized chunks which you can work on. Understand procrastination and deal with it as it will steal your time and delay you in completing your PhD. Social support is important on your PhD journey—do not be alone.

Life has a way of interrupting the best made plans; expect this to happen and adjust your plans accordingly and keep chipping away at your PhD. Make sure to look after yourself along the way to your PhD. Build good stress busting practices such as exercise and good diet into your daily routine. Avoid excessive consumption of alcohol and caffeine. Reward progress on your PhD with time spent on hobbies, leisure and with family and friends. Once you build a good work routine and gain momentum on your PhD keep at it. Avoid stopping for long periods and then re-starting, as it is much easier to keep going once you get started.

Chapter Five

Completing the PhD, Graduation & Beyond

The End Game

There comes a point in the PhD when your thoughts are no longer going back and forth between should I quit or complete my PhD. Even up to quite late in the PhD process I entertained thoughts of quitting. Of course these were distracting, useless and unhelpful thoughts. It is much better to make a decision to continue or not and then act accordingly rather than constantly debating the issue in your mind. However, there comes a point where the end is actually in sight and quitting is out of the question.

As mentioned previously, I was fortunate that I got a short-term job at the university where I was registered as a student. The job was to cover a staff member who was on maternity leave for six months. Being in an academic environment and supervising the theses of undergraduate students was a great motivator to propel me to complete my PhD. It was the lucky break that I needed to accelerate my completion of the PhD. I was regularly meeting my PhD supervisor who was also head of the section in the university where I was working. The end result was that I knuckled down and grasped the opportunity with both hands and worked hard to finish my thesis.

There are times when progress on your PhD can be slow. However, this was a time for me when I had a sense that the end of the PhD was near. My confidence grew that I was actually going to complete the PhD and I worked harder than ever. As the saying goes, there was light at the end of the tunnel. As a result I made very good progress on my thesis in the five months before submission. I started work at the university in January and submitted my PhD thesis in May. It was such a great feeling when my supervisor signed off on my thesis as being ready for examination, I printed and soft bound it and I submitted the thesis to the university.

After years of work on your PhD (six years in my case) you go home after submission and don't have to work on your PhD anymore. It's like being released from a prison of sorts. All of a sudden you have all this free time! Submitting my PhD thesis also meant that the fees clock was now stopped. At my university once you submit the thesis for examination you don't pay any more fees, and that was an immense relief in itself. I had to use a credit card to borrow money to pay my fees balance on submission of my thesis as money was so tight. In addition, fees had increased rapidly in the final years of my PhD as a result of austerity/budget cuts in Ireland. Therefore, to be out from under the yoke of fees was a huge relief. After submission of my PhD thesis all I had to do was wait for my Viva Voce exam and then defend my thesis, as the bulk of the work was now done.

The Viva Voce

Viva voce is a Latin phrase literally meaning "with living voice," but most often interpreted as "by word of mouth." It is essentially an oral examination in which you 'defend' your thesis. The purpose of the Viva is to establish that your work is of a sufficiently high standard to merit the award of the degree for which it is submitted. In order to be awarded a research degree, the thesis should demonstrate an original contribution to knowledge and contain work which is deemed worthy of publication. For my Viva Voce examination I was examined by a panel which included one internal examiner and one external examiner. In addition, there was an academic chairing the discussion, and my supervisor was also present (but not part of the panel) in the capacity of an observer only.

Each country and different institutions will have their own way of conducting the examinations process for a PhD and the Viva Voce. What I am describing here happened in the National University of Ireland. Regulations can also change over time and it is important that you check the requirements in the institution where you are registered as a student. Under the Irish system the Viva Voce examination happens in private. This is similar to what happens in the United Kingdom. In Australia an oral defence of the thesis is not the norm. In continental European countries such as Holland and Germany, for example, you have to present your thesis in a public and formal defence. In the U.S.

and Canada, the majority of universities require an oral defence of a written dissertation, which is usually open to the public. The same situation exists in most Asian and African countries.

My own particular experience was of the Irish system and the aim of the Irish Viva Voce examination is to provide an opportunity for the Examiners to question the candidate on aspects of the thesis. It is designed to assess the quality of the thesis and to elicit information on any or all of the following issues:

1. Explanation of the structure of the thesis.
2. Justification for the inclusion or exclusion of material.
3. Explanation for and justification of the use of particular research methods and techniques.
4. Verification that the thesis is the candidate's own work.
5. Defence of the originality of the thesis.
6. Clarification of any points of ambiguity within the thesis.
7. Justification for the conceptual approach taken in the thesis.
8. The depth of knowledge of the contextual background to the subject of the thesis.

Under the Irish examination system the Viva Voce can have one of the following outcomes:

- Award PhD - no corrections to the thesis required
- Award PhD - subject to minor corrections
- Revise thesis and submit for re-examination

- That the PhD not be awarded

If successful, the most likely outcome is the second option—"Award PhD subject to minor revisions..." Being awarded a PhD with no corrections required is less common. A good supervisor will not allow you to submit a thesis for examination which is likely to fail. It is important to listen to your supervisor when he or she asks you for what may seem like endless revisions and to address weaknesses in the thesis before allowing you to submit. Your supervisor will have a good idea if your thesis is up to the required standard and should not allow you to proceed to examination before reaching this standard. Having a good supervisor with high standards meant that my own Viva examination went smoothly. The outcome of my Viva was to award a PhD subject to minor corrections. My memory of the Viva examination was generally positive—after all, I had spent six years researching my topic. The discussion focussed on giving clarifications to my examiners and discussing some minor improvements. Making these minor corrections took me about four weeks. Once I received approval that the corrections had been made correctly I was then able to print and bind copies of my final thesis and submit to the university (what a relief!).

So you got your PhD— What Next?

"Save for the very best, career paths are not clearly evident for most doctoral students."

- Irish University Association, 2004

Life's path often looks more like a maze than a straight line—here I am back at the beginning trying to figure out the benefits of doing a PhD while I have already finished! I am back to contemplating why I did the PhD in the first place, what I am going to do next and how the PhD is going to be useful to me. I am investigating career options now but should have done this in a more thorough and systematic way before committing to do the PhD! This should have been a key aspect of my decision to do a PhD, but unfortunately, it was not. When I registered for my PhD in 2006, I didn't think much about so far off an issue as what I would do after I got the PhD or issues of future income earning potential with a PhD. When I started the PhD it seemed like an exciting adventure. I had an initial three years of funding and I cared only about my subject and contributing to the frontiers of knowledge on my subject. When I started the PhD I was also very uncertain if I would be capable of doing the PhD at all, or if I would ever finish with a PhD, so there was no point thinking ahead to what I would do after completing my PhD. Looking back, I realise I should have made a cold, calculated decision whether or not to do a PhD and been clear about what I wanted from it in terms of a future career and income.

Some important questions I should have answered for myself before embarking on my PhD journey are:

- What happens to people who complete PhDs?
- Where do they go?
- What do they do?
- What are the career prospects of people with PhDs?
- How much do PhD graduates earn?

- What is my career goal?
- Why do I need to get a PhD and how will it help me achieve my career goal?
- Is being over-qualified for some jobs a problem?

Careers for PhD holders

The first and most obvious career for a PhD holder is academic. However, there has been a substantial increase in the number of PhDs awarded compared, for example, to the 1960s, when universities were expanding and most PhD's could find an academic job. According to an article published in the Economist magazine (2010), titled 'The Disposable Academic - Why Doing a PhD is often a Waste of Time,' there is today an oversupply of PhDs. A doctorate is designed as training for a job in academia; however, the number of PhD positions is unrelated to the number of job openings (America produced more than 100,000 doctoral degrees between 2005 and 2009 while there were just 16,000 new professorships during the same period).

According to a report by the Academy of Science for South Africa (ASSA, 2010), between 1991 and 2004, China had an 817% rate of increase in PhD production, increasing the number of PhDs granted from 2,556 to 23,446. Around 50,000 people graduated with doctorates in China across all disciplines in 2009 (Cyranoski et al., 2011). In the 13 years between 1991 and 2004 the UK had an 82% increase in the number of PhDs granted from 8,390 to 15,260. Other countries cited in the ASSA report with substantial increases in their number of PhD graduates include Japan, Taiwan, South Korea and Australia. In Ireland, the OECD review of Higher Education, conducted in 2004, recommended that Ireland double its PhD output. By

2006 Ireland had increased the number of PhD graduates to 230 per million of population (a 37% increase). According to Deloitte (2010), the number of new doctoral graduates in the European Union 27 (number of member countries from 1 January 2007 - 30 June 2013) increased from 82,705 in 2001 to around 115,000 in 2010.

All of this means more and more competition for academic jobs and hence the need for increasing numbers of PhD graduates to work outside academia. In Ireland about 50% of Irish students move directly out of academia on completion of their PhD, yet the traditional European PhD is still often seen as tailored to the research needs of academia (Irish Universities Association, 2004). Ireland's Strategy for Science Technology and Innovation is consistent with public policies in many other countries, which encourage doctoral holders to seek careers in enterprise and also in public policy research. Given that there are too few academic jobs this approach seems the only option.

The skills and attributes the PhD experience confers are likely transferable across a broad range of professional careers. In the US notable PhD holders involved in non-academic roles include:

- Condoleezza Rice, former US Secretary of State
- Brian May, Guitarist with Queen
- Bill Cosby, American comedian
- Ben Bernanke, Chairman of the US Federal Reserve

(Source: http://www.euraxess.ie/phd/page.aspx?SP=205)

Many PhD holders pursue highly successful and rewarding non-academic careers as shown above. However, I am not sure how much the PhD actually helped the above people achieve their success! Perhaps the PhD was just a distraction to their true calling? It is not clear that spending years securing this high level qualification (a PhD) is worth it for a job as, for example, a high-school teacher (Cyranoski, 2011). It is important that prospective PhD students enter PhD programmes with their eyes wide open to the opportunities—or lack of them—at the end.

Another aspect of this discussion is the quality of academic jobs on offer. In the USA the number of tenured posts in academia is now down to 30% of positions (Gallagher, 2012 p. 26). Tenure in education is a guarantee of the permanence of a college or university teacher's position, awarded upon successful completion of a probationary period. Tenure is designed to make a teaching career more attractive by providing job security; by protecting the teacher's position, tenure also tends to enforce academic freedom. The majority of PhD graduates will therefore not secure full-time academic positions, even if this is the dominant goal motivating students to seek these degrees. The education offered to students in PhD programs should accommodate this reality. Institutions should be more open with students about attrition rates and the labour outcomes of doctoral graduates, especially for those who end up in positions other than the traditional academic ones (Maldonado et al., 2013).

Reflections on my Post PhD Career

Fast forward seven years after starting my PhD, and as I write these words my PhD certificate is proudly (?) hanging on the wall over my desk. I am finally a free man again after six years of PhD study. I had this monkey on my back for six years, and I feel relieved to be finished. I can now focus on doing other things without feeling I have this massive project to chip away at! I can earn money, take the kids to a movie and watch TV if I want. Since completing my PhD I have started learning the guitar and have taken up running. I am also learning two new languages—Portuguese and Chinese. When at work I can focus on my work. I now have the PhD completed and there is no more pain associated with it. I am finished and I have my PhD in the bag. The PhD is not going to be a burden to me anymore, and my PhD hopefully will contribute positively to the rest of my life. However, the work I am currently doing does not require a PhD (I am over-qualified for the position), and I am working at a job which is in many ways unrelated to my specific expertise and PhD research. I am earning the equivalent of the average industrial wage in Ireland. My PhD is very specialised and is not particularly relevant or useful in Ireland. It is, in fact, relevant and useful in Africa where I did my PhD research, but I am, of course, not there anymore having shifted continent! I cannot use my specialist knowledge/expertise to any extent in Ireland where I am living, and I think my current wage reflects this.

After reading a book by Susan Basalla and Maggie Debelius titled, *So What are You Going to Do with That*, I realised that my situation of having to move away from my area of specialisation is not unusual. For example, people with PhDs in the humanities with very narrow topics on history or English who move outside academia are also moving away from their areas of expertise. I think you have to look beyond the subject matter of your PhD to the process itself. When thinking of a career for a PhD graduate you have to think of not just the area of expertise but you have to think of the critical thinking research skills that are transferable to so many jobs. The real value is *learning how to learn,* which can now be applied to other subject areas related to any future employment. To quote the above book: *"...the specific content of your dissertation is of little interest or value to most people outside academia. If you begin your job search with the idea that you are an expert on a particular topic seeking a place to ply your trade, you are likely to fail. What is valuable about your dissertation is the process of writing it, not the product itself..."* (Basalla & Debelius, 2007, pg. 434).

As I examine my own career I realise now that I do not have to be defined by the subject matter of my PhD; I can apply the skills and attitudes learned from the PhD process to any career direction of my choosing. This realisation is hugely liberating and frees me now to choose a new direction in my career and not feel trapped by past career decisions which are no longer relevant.

As regards a PhD making you over-qualified for some jobs, I think this may be possible, but it is important to take each position you are applying for as a separate case. You will be dealing with different people doing the hiring with different fears and expectations. If you are overqualified for a job the person doing the hiring may fear that you will get bored quickly and leave at the first opportunity. They may also fear that you will have high salary expectations. They may also feel threatened by your PhD if you have a higher qualification than them. Try to understand it from their point of view and pre-empt their fears.

Do I want to be a researcher? I wrote one research paper—will I write another? Looking at the blogs of some researchers/academics, there is a list of research publications as long as your arm! I don't foresee myself ever writing more than the odd research paper unless it is part of my job (such as a university position) and I am required to do it! Why? Writing academic papers is very demanding.

In summary, two years post completing my PhD I am currently working outside academia and outside my area of expertise and earning the average industrial wage in my country. How exactly the PhD will help my career going forward is not clear to me at this stage post my PhD. However, I do realise now that the process of doing the PhD has taught me valuable skills and attitudes which I can use going forward to enhance my career. On reflection, before I choose to embark on doing my PhD I should have been much clearer on how the PhD was going to be a stepping stone to a particular desired career path rather than looking at the PhD as being an end in itself.

Earning potential of people with PhDs

A study presented in the *Journal of Higher Education Policy and Management* by Bernard Casey (Casey, 2009) examined the value of doing a PhD to the individual and to society as a whole. The analysis is from the economic perspective and concludes that all PhDs are not the same. Casey references research by O'Leary and Sloane (2005) which shows that British men with a bachelor's degree earn over 20% more than those who could have gone to university but chose not to, while women who studied earned over 35% more than the equivalent comparator. Studying to a higher level brings further returns; however, the higher the level you go, declining returns set in. Men with a master's degree earn 29% more than the base, while women earn 55% more than the base. Obtaining a PhD raises the gap further—men with a PhD earn 31% more than the base and women 60% more than the base. However, the returns from doing a PhD are different depending on the subject studied. In some subjects the premium for a PhD disappears completely. PhDs in maths and computing, social sciences and languages earn no more than those with master's degrees. The premium for a PhD is actually smaller than for a master's degree in engineering and technology, architecture and education. Only in medicine, other sciences, and business and financial studies is it high enough to be worthwhile. Over all subjects, a PhD commands only a 3% premium over a master's degree. There are arguments, however, that the production of PhDs benefits wider society in that the acquisition of PhDs generates and transfers knowledge that the rest of society can benefit from (Casey, 2009).

In Canada many of the academic positions are taken up by postdocs. Postdocs are people who have completed PhDs who are on contract and engaged in postdoctoral research. Postdoctoral research is scholarly research conducted by a person who has completed doctoral studies, and they typically perform research under the supervision and mentorship of a more senior researcher. In Canada 80% of postdocs earn $38,600 or less per year before tax—the average salary of a construction worker (Economist, 2010).

A study by the Higher Education Authority in Ireland (2013 B) revealed that of those PhD graduates in employment for whom salary information was returned:

- 11% were earning under €25,000
- 59% were earning between €25,000 and €45,000
- 30% were earning over €45,000

According to the CSO data the average annual industrial wage in Ireland was about €43,102 in 2012. Therefore, doing a PhD was not an automatic ticket to a high salary, and a significant proportion of PhD holders were in low paid work.

One OECD study (Auriol, 2010) shows that five years after receiving their degrees, more than 60% of PhDs in Slovakia and more than 45% in Belgium, the Czech Republic, Germany and Spain were still on temporary contracts. Many were postdocs. Nearly one-third of Austria's PhD graduates take jobs unrelated to their degrees. In Germany 13% of all PhD graduates end up in lowly occupations. In the Netherlands the proportion is 21%.

Therefore, if you think that doing a PhD will automatically substantially increase your earning potential you need to think again, because as presented above, there may be little or no increase in earning potential as a result of doing a PhD (with variations depending on subject area and gender differences). I think it is also worth referencing here research by Pfeffer and Fong (2002) on the value of Masters in Business Administration (MBA) degrees. Research on graduates with MBAs (a highly valued credential) revealed that neither possessing an MBA degree nor grades earned in courses correlate with career success. I think the same may apply to having a PhD. In other words, do not expect your career to fall into place once you have completed a PhD. Rather, see the PhD as a stepping stone to your desired future and be clear on what that desired future is. Having a PhD is a means to an end and not an end in itself.

The research presented above was something I was totally unaware of when I was beginning and working on my PhD. I was too busy focussing on getting my PhD to think of these important higher level issues! I had a vague notion that:

1. All PhDs were pretty much the same, and

2. Having a PhD would automatically increase my earning potential.

It just seemed logical to me that the higher my qualifications then the more pay I could command. It is best to be aware that having a PhD is not an automatic ticket to a good, well-paid job before deciding to do a PhD so that you can make a better informed decision before deciding to begin! However, a narrow focus on the economic benefits and costs of doing a PhD is also insufficient. We need to look beyond economics. Some of the other benefits and costs of doing a PhD are explored in this book. For example, doing a PhD can teach you how to persevere and succeed while tackling a difficult goal (a very valuable skill). The costs of doing a PhD are also far greater than monetary costs alone. For example, the time input required to complete a PhD and the opportunity cost of not having time to spend with family and friends.

Expectations on completing the PhD

For most jobs a PhD is unnecessary, and a large proportion of people with PhDs end up working outside academia, many not very well paid (like me!). According to Maldonado et al. (2013), *"completing a PhD is not now—nor has it ever been—a guaranteed path to a lucrative end, and its general value has come under increasing scrutiny in recent years."*

Using the title 'Dr.' outside academia has a hint of self-importance to it, and you are likely to avoid using the title. I certainly do not use it. Another reflection on having a PhD and careers is related to expectations. I have a wife, children, relatives and friends who have seen me struggle for six years on my doctorate. They witnessed my graduation with all the pomp and ceremony, music and red robes. Now that I have struggled and attained this qualification and I am still in an ordinary job earning the average industrial wage in Ireland, the question in my mind—and I imagine in the mind of others—is why did I bother? As a family man I do feel that I should be able to give my family a better life as a result of my PhD struggles; after all, they sacrificed and struggled with me along the way. It is frustrating that so far I have been unable to deliver a better life for my family as a result of completing my PhD. However, the pain of doing the PhD is now over, so perhaps the rewards are yet to come. Another personal expectation is that I should be able to make more meaningful contributions in my work since I have a PhD. I think others expect it, but it doesn't mean that by my having a PhD that what I say will be better/more intelligent etc. or even that I will know what to contribute at all. Outside my area of expertise, my knowledge is just like anyone else's, and I may not be able to contribute more than if I did not have a PhD. I sometimes, therefore, do not want to tell people that I have a PhD because it creates an expectation that I might know more, when I actually don't. However, I may also have a touch of the imposter syndrome described in the next section!

Imposter Syndrome

"The trouble with the world is that the stupid are cocksure and the intelligent are full of doubt."

- Bertrand Russell

The impostor syndrome is the feeling that you're a fraud, and any day now you'll be exposed. Research shows that it tends to affect women more than men (Clance and Imes, 1978). It is presumably even more common than surveys suggest, as it is not the kind of thing to which people like to admit. It's a classic case of "comparing your insides with other people's outsides..." You have access only to your own self-doubt, so you wrongly conclude it's more justified than anyone else's. I had never heard of this syndrome until writing this book; however, I think I am suffering from Imposter Syndrome to some extent. I have a bachelor's degree, two masters' degrees and a PhD, and I feel like a fraud in some way. I feel uncomfortable using my new title "Doctor." I have a feeling that perhaps I am not good enough to be using the title. I am naturally an introverted person and don't enjoy being the focus of the attention of others. I imagine people thinking, 'look at him, he has a PhD and he is not very smart—how did he get a PhD?' I think it takes courage to put yourself up there as a source of expertise and to feel exposed and vulnerable. You need to carry the title; you are saying, here I am, a source of expertise and knowledge. You are implying that because you are using the title 'Doctor' that you may know more than others, and to me this is scary as I probably don't know more—on my specialism, African beekeeping, perhaps, but outside my area of expertise it is likely I do not know more!

Sunk Costs in Careers

As already discussed in this book, the sunk cost effect is the tendency to keep doing something that doesn't make sense anymore, just because of how much you've already paid for it. You have spent years of your life and a lot of money to get your PhD. However, on finishing you know in your heart and soul that this area of work or sector is not for you for whatever reason. It is very hard to walk away after how much you have invested in your current career. It is just the way life is that things do not go according to plan for whatever reason—poor planning, altered circumstances, bad luck. We have to decide to do something different or stick with our original plan. In my own case I invested years of my life studying and working on African bees. I have just completed my PhD on African beekeeping. However, my circumstances have now changed. I am now living in Ireland where there is little use for my expertise. The sunk costs are large—years of effort and experience. I cannot ever get those years and money invested in my PhD back again. I have to move forward from where I am now and in many ways start over and redefine myself.

Being aware of this bias is very helpful as it gives me the freedom to choose a new path for myself going forward. The sunk cost bias makes it hard to admit something is not working. Because of the large investment of time and resources in my PhD it is hard to admit that perhaps this was the wrong path for me. It is hard to admit to mistakes. However, I have realised that I do not have to be defined by my PhD just because of the sunk costs involved in attaining it. I have invested six years of my life and considerable funds, but I do not have to allow the PhD to define me or corral me into pursuing a certain career path, such as being an academic. In hindsight, I realise that my doing a PhD may have been a mistake. However, I can cut my losses and start over; I can begin again with a blank canvas from where I am today and choose a new path forward for my career and my life. I can take the valuable transferable skills I learned from the process of doing the PhD, such as critical thinking and learning how to learn, and apply these skills to a new career direction. (See Bornstein and Chapman (1995) for further discussion on sunk costs.)

"Live out of your imagination, not your history."

- Stephen Covey

Higher education is changing

I think that it is important to consider that we live in an era of rapid change and this change is also affecting higher education. Change has always been with us, but it's the pace of change at the moment which is really striking. There are rapid ongoing advances in many fields, and in particular, in technology and communications. The growth of the popularity of the internet in the 1990s has brought many changes and new ways of communicating and doing things. Access to information and opportunities to learn have never been as great as they are today.

A recent innovation has been the advent of Massive Open Online Courses (MOOCs). There are many of these courses run by top universities online for free. I have completed a number of these free MOOCs, and the quality of tuition through online interaction using videos, documents and online quizzes is very high. Students can access the world's top lecturers in 'virtual' universities for free or modest costs, yet the more traditional universities—for example in Ireland—are continually increasing fees. There are also new ways of learning which combine online and offline learning. A new phenomenon known as 'Flip Learning' is emerging. The traditional practice has been to lecture to students and then they complete assignments at home. Now students can watch the lecture at home and come to class to do their homework under the guidance of the lecturer—the lecturer then becomes more of a facilitator of learning. This turns on its head the traditional model of teaching. There is a democratisation of knowledge and how we access knowledge. Some commentators suggest that formal qualifications such as degrees are becoming less relevant as employers find new ways to identify and evaluate new employees using online portfolios and communities of practice.

Is the PhD still relevant?

As we have discussed earlier in this chapter there has been a major increase in the supply of PhD graduates in recent years forcing many PhD graduates to seek careers outside academia. There are no longer enough academic jobs and many lecturing jobs have become part-time. Some commentators such a Mark C. Taylor, a professor at Colombia University in the US, argue that the PhD system is broken:

"The system of PhD education in the United States and many other countries is broken and unsustainable, and needs to be reconceived. In many fields, it creates only a cruel fantasy of future employment that promotes the self-interest of faculty members at the expense of students. The reality is that there are very few jobs for people who might have spent up to 12 years on their degrees." (Taylor, 2011).

If we take Canada as an example, about 50% of those who enter PhD programs in the humanities do not complete. Those who do complete their PhDs take seven years on average to finish. Of those who do receive the degree, only about 20%-30% secure positions in colleges and universities (McGill University, 2013).

When I reflect on my own just completed PhD, it was the traditional model of PhD where you study for years under the apprenticeship of an academic supervisor. As I can see now, with the increasing number of PhD graduates and shrinking opportunities in academia, the chances of my finding a job in academia are small. I would have benefited more from a broader doctoral training leading to a variety of career paths instead of training for a job in academia when I will most likely not be an academic. When I was a PhD student I did not think about what I would do after completing my PhD because I was totally absorbed by the PhD itself and was unable to think about what could possibly come next.

If you want to be a researcher you don't have to have a PhD. You can write and submit research papers and have them published and in the process build up a name for yourself as a researcher.

However, the best way to answer the question posed by the heading of this section is to ask yourself is the PhD relevant to you and will it help you to achieve your career goals. If not, then steer clear, unless of course you enjoy inflicting pain on yourself!

Chapter Five summary

There comes a point where the end of the PhD is finally in sight and, hopefully, you will get a wind at your back which propels you to the completion of your PhD. A good supervisor will not allow you to submit a thesis which is likely to be rejected by your examiners. Therefore, listen carefully to your supervisor when he/she asks you to make what seem like endless changes. All the work you have put in and edits and revisions suggested by your supervisor will make your Viva Voce exam go more smoothly. In any case, during your Viva Voce exam you are discussing your research—something you will be very familiar with after years of effort.

Once you have completed your PhD you will be faced with the big question—what next? This moment will arrive if you work consistently on your PhD, and you need to be planning for your career post your PhD before you decide to start your PhD and also during the PhD itself. In recent years there has been a major increase in the supply of PhD graduates around the world, so having a PhD is no longer as exclusive as it once was. At the same time there are fewer academic jobs, which means that the majority of PhD graduates will most likely not secure full-time academic positions. The financial returns from getting a PhD depend on the subject area studied, and over all subjects a PhD commands on average only a 3% premium over a master's degree, and for certain subjects there is no premium at all. Having a PhD will not automatically substantially increase your earning potential, and research from different countries shows that many PhD graduates end up in poorly paid jobs.

Beware of the impostor syndrome, which is the feeling that you're a fraud, you don't really deserve your PhD and any day now you'll be exposed. The imposter syndrome can hold you back in your career and is a classic case of comparing your insides to other people's outsides.

You will have struggled for years doing a PhD and both you and your loved ones/family will have made many sacrifices of time and money to get to this point of having the PhD completed. Having achieved your PhD they will expect you to reap the rewards from your years of study. In many cases, however, the rewards will not be forthcoming.

Having invested so much in getting a PhD in a particular subject area, it can be difficult to change course and start over again doing something different in your career due to the amount of money and effort invested in getting your PhD—the sunk cost effect. However, you can start over afresh and move in a new direction in your career at any moment, whether you are in the course of getting a PhD or have already completed. When considering a career change, focus on the valuable transferable skills learned from the PhD process itself which can be applied to your new career as opposed to feeling tied to your particular subject area.

The context of higher education is changing rapidly and there are more ways to access education and knowledge online than ever before. Whether or not the PhD is still relevant in today's world is a question which must be answered by each individual in relation to their own specific career goals.

Chapter Six

Conclusion

"If you will be hard on yourself, life will be easy on you. But if you insist upon being easy on yourself, life is going to be very hard on you."

- Zig Ziglar, American Motivational Speaker

In this chapter, the final chapter, key points made in this book are summarised and conclusions drawn from them. The conclusions are largely based on my own personal experience of doing a PhD and reflections on the process, having struggled throughout the PhD, stuck with it and successfully completed my PhD in the end.

What I learned from the PhD process

For me, doing a PhD was a really large and difficult personal goal. As I mentioned in Chapter Two, doing a PhD was a personal BHAG (Big Hairy Audacious Goal). Getting my PhD was a personal proverbial mountain I chose to climb. Some people set particular challenges for themselves such as running a marathon, long distance swimming, climbing a difficult mountain or doing an Ironman event—I set doing a PhD as a personal challenge. In this section I want to summarise what I learned from the PhD process.

"What you get by achieving your goals is not as important as what you become by achieving your goals."

- Henry David Thoreau, American Philosopher

You are the boss

At the end of the day this is your PhD project and your life. In your project, be the captain of your ship. The buck stops with you. Success or failure is ultimately on your shoulders. Nobody else can do this for you. Pearce Flannery, who is an Irish business coach, motivational speaker and author of the book, *Grabbing the Oyster*, puts it more bluntly. He says you have to learn to 'Kick you own arse!' Push yourself. The quicker you get this PhD done then the quicker you will get the monkey off your back!

Develop grit—learn to persist

Doing a PhD is about learning to keep going, keep struggling, not to give up and not become despondent in the face of failure over a long-term project (provided you are sure achieving a PhD is the right goal for you—if not, then 'let go'—see Chapter Four for a discussion on when its okay to quit). A PhD is a marathon and not a sprint—you are in this for the long hall. It will take you years to complete a PhD. When you fall down, you get back up—keep going, persevere over a long time, encounter problems and overcome them, experience failure and mistakes and correct them until you get to the final victory. Don't worry if your PhD appears to be a mess and off track. Keep going—failure is not a permanent condition. Developing a growth mindset is really helpful to developing grit. *A growth mindset is a belief that the ability to learn is not fixed and it can change with your effort.* When I look back at my PhD I was off track for most of the time. My PhD was in crisis and behind most of the time. However, I stuck with it and got there in the end. Once you make daily small progress you will get there—do something on your PhD no matter how small each day, keep the forward momentum and don't panic.

Manage your time well and finish fast

Your PhD will expand to fill the time you give it! Your main objective is to focus on getting this monkey off your back as soon as possible. If you allow it, this project will expand and could take years longer than needed. Get it done as quickly as possible. The longer you spend on the PhD the more that can go wrong, and unexpected events arise to throw you off track. In my own case I had to change countries and careers and funds were drying up at the end. All of these were unforeseen when I started my PhD. My mistake was to lose focus and go down rabbit trails, such as writing a book in the middle of my PhD. As a consequence, it took me six years to complete my PhD—perhaps up to two years longer than necessary to comfortably complete the PhD. The lesson I learned was to plan well and make sure you complete your PhD in the shortest time possible. As far as the outside world is concerned there are only two types of PhD dissertation—finished and unfinished, so get it finished as fast as possible. If you do get delayed stop worrying, start work on it today, keep going and get back on track!

Plan well

Taking the time to read this and other books about doing a PhD is very important. Talk to people who have done or are doing a PhD and get their advice. Act on lessons learned from those who have gone before you—why repeat the mistakes of others? If you take the time to do this you will go into the PhD with your eyes open and be clear on potential pitfalls and how to avoid them.

Make an overview plan of your PhD from start to finish and develop key milestones which you need to achieve along the way. Discuss and agree this plan with your supervisor(s). Visualise yourself achieving key PhD milestones and the end of your PhD, such as visualising yourself handing in your completed thesis or your graduation ceremony. The danger is that you can lose sight of the big picture of what you are aiming for and your intermediate goals on the way to PhD success. Celebrate as you achieve key milestones along the way and reward yourself—you deserve it.

Tiny changes mean huge results

I mentioned in Chapter Three reading a book titled *Write Your Dissertation in Fifteen Minutes a Day,* by Joan Bolker. I don't remember much of the book but the title stuck in my mind. That is because the message is to do at least a little every day and you will get there in the end. Of course 15 minutes may not be enough; however, when you start work on your PhD you will find that once you have done your 15 minutes you will want to continue. The hardest thing is to start on anything, so once you begin you get momentum. It's a way to overcome writer's block. I have written this book using a similar strategy by writing for only 30 minutes most days—over time this small investment of time each day has resulted in a complete book.

Work hard

During my PhD I learned to work hard and learned to cope with setbacks. I believe these are invaluable skills for any kind of success in life. You cannot get a PhD without hard work. You must put in the time and effort. It does not matter how smart you are, hard work is a must if you want to be successful and earn a PhD. You need to develop a mindset of hard work and accepting and learning from failure—a growth mindset, as discussed in the book, *Mindset—The New Psychology of Success*, by Carol Dweck. Don't forget to play hard as well when you are taking a break!

Develop good habits

"Sow a thought and you reap an action; sow an act and you reap a habit; sow a habit and you reap a character; sow a character and you reap a destiny."

- Ralph Waldo Emerson, American Poet

A PhD is a marathon and not a sprint, so it is not the epic all-nighters that are needed but a sustained investment of time every day. Our habits define us over the long term and the results that we get. Be conscious and fully aware of your habitual behaviour. What repeating patterns of behaviour do you have? It often surprises me when I see people acting out the same repeating patterns of behaviour or ways of thinking as evidenced by what they say and being completely unaware of it. What you think and do every day counts. You can only ever do your PhD in the *now*—today. Manage your time well. You need to develop habits which support you getting your PhD. A key habit I developed was getting up at 5:00 a.m. in the morning. Another key habit I cultivated was 'eating the frog for breakfast'—doing the thing I most disliked first thing in the morning. Other key habits were to get to bed early and get plenty of rest, conduct daily and weekly reviews and planning sessions to keep me on track, regular exercise and a healthy diet. As mentioned in Chapter Three, you can use a smartphone app to monitor and keep track of habits.

Manage stress

A 2006 mental health report by the University of California acknowledged that graduate students are *"a population at higher risk for mental health concerns. The level of stress for graduate students is magnified by their relative isolation from the broader components of campus life, the intense academic pressures of their advanced studies, and the increased presence of family and financial obligations."* (Dimsdale & Young, 2006). Stress is a reality and you need to build stress mitigation into your daily routine. Manage stress by exercising daily. Maintain a healthy diet and avoid excessive consumption of caffeine and alcohol. Control negative self-talk using meditation. After work on your PhD is done, switch off and relax—do something different—reward yourself and celebrate every time you achieve a mini goal. Plan well so you know where you are on your PhD journey. Reach out to others if your PhD is stressing you—a problem shared is a problem halved.

You are intelligent enough

In order to get a PhD you don't have to be the most intelligent person in your year or academically brilliant. You just have to be intelligent enough—that's all! Beyond a certain threshold, intelligence is no longer the key success factor; other factors come into play, such as hard work and perseverance (there is a good discussion of this concept in the book, *Outliers*, by Malcolm Gladwell (Gladwell, 2008). The good news is that if you are contemplating doing, or are accepted into a PhD programme, then you are already intelligent enough to get your PhD. You no longer have to contemplate whether or not you are really smart enough to get a PhD. Tell the little voice in your head known as the 'inner critic' to shut up and repeat to yourself 'I am start enough!' Negative thoughts like 'I am not smart enough to get a PhD' or 'I will never finish this' are like driving a car with the handbrake on—they just slow you down. These are useless, time wasting thoughts and keep you from focussing on the work at hand and delay progress on completing your PhD. The thought 'I am not good enough' is self-fulfilling—delete it from your mind. You are good enough and you can do it! Focus on what you can do next. Each small action is progress towards the day you will finish!

Begin again each day

If you go off track with your PhD, it is okay. For example, you miss a few days, weeks or months (or in my case a year!) when you should have worked on your PhD. Forget feeling guilty and depressed. Just start work again on your PhD now. Feeling guilty can make us not restart work on our PhD. All of us fall down from time to time; it's okay—we are human. The important thing is to get back up again and start over again working on your PhD. Every day is a new beginning irrespective of what has happened up to that point.

"I am glad you make a fresh beginning daily; there is no better means of attaining… than by continually beginning again."

- St. Francis de Sales

Think about life after the PhD

In some ways my own PhD is a monument to lack of planning in my own life. I did not put enough careful thought and planning into it before embarking on my PhD journey. What are your longer term plans and goals? Is doing a PhD necessary for you to achieve your goals? If it's not necessary then why do a PhD? I had a vague notion that I wanted to be an expert in my field and the PhD would be the means to deepen my expertise. However, as I write I am no longer working in that area of expertise. I am also not working in academia. You must take a longer-term perspective on what you want to be and who you wish to become.

Yes, there is life after doing a PhD, and if you have decided to go ahead and do a PhD then you will likely get to the stage I am at now (life after completing the PhD). You will get to this stage if you make consistent sustained effort working on your PhD. I never thought about life after the PhD because I was so consumed by the PhD itself that I thought I would never get here! When I started my PhD I was unaware of the career prospects of graduates—my head was in the sand. It just seemed too far down the road to contemplate what I would do after my PhD. What I have learned is that a PhD is not a dream ticket and that your life will not be sorted out once you get your PhD completed. We cannot be blinded by the few who are very successful. What about all the others who have PhDs? The problem is that PhD students may focus so much on the immediate goal to get the PhD that we cannot see or think beyond that—this is natural. However, we must force ourselves to look beyond the PhD. We cannot assume that everything will work out. We can fool ourselves into believing that the PhD is a magic bullet and our lives will be sorted once we get our PhDs.

Do some people who have PhDs have problems paying the bills or struggle to get a job or struggles in their job? Yes! We cannot make assumptions that everything will work out automatically. Before you even start a PhD you need to carefully consider where you want to go with your career and how having a PhD will support you to reach your ultimate goal. You need to make sure that your future plans are as realistic as possible. If you have already started a PhD you need to keep an eye on the future and what you want to do when your PhD is completed. Invest in your future—build your network, expand activities and skills based on where you want to find yourself at the end of your PhD.

You need a good team

Don't underestimate the power of your team or the people around you who will support you in getting your PhD. First of all, your main supervisor, in particular, is critical to success or failure. This one decision alone—which supervisor you choose—can determine if you succeed or fail at your PhD.

Choose a supervisor with care and talk to current and past students to find out what your potential supervisor is really like. Once you have found a good supervisor, discuss mutual expectations about supervision with him or her.

Support of friends and family is also crucial. In particular, close family, as they will share the burden of your PhD. Your time will be constrained over a number of years and there will be financial implications due to direct expenditure on the PhD as well as opportunity costs of work you cannot take up because you are too busy on the PhD. Organise peer support as well. Get to know your fellow PhD students—they are the ones who really understand what you are going through. Meet your fellow PhD students on a regular basis and share your PhD frustrations. I spent most of my PhD working in isolation from other PhD students, and I do not recommend that.

It was only in the latter stages of my PhD that I met and shared with my fellow PhD students, and it felt good to be finally understood and learn that what I was going through was not unique to me alone! Make use of all available sources of support. For example, there may be a group of PhD students who meet regularly, or the institution may have other supports such as counselling and guidance services available to PhD students. Ensure that you know what these supports are and be ready to avail of them if needed.

Some good luck also helps

I had some good luck which helped me to complete my PhD. I happened to choose a very good PhD supervisor, which was more to do with luck than my own careful analysis of potential supervisors. Towards the end of my PhD I also worked in an academic position for the university where I was registered as a student, and being in this academic environment helped me to complete my PhD. However, I also had my fair share of challenges along the way and kept going. Grit, or the ability to keep going in the face of adversity, puts you in the position to take advantage of lady luck when she appears! Don't leave everything to luck, but put yourself in a good position to take advantage of lucky breaks when they arise. Take control of your PhD through careful planning.

> *"Luck is what happens when preparation meets opportunity."*
>
> - Seneca, Roman Philosopher

How I have benefited by doing a PhD

Writing this section of the book was really interesting for me. Much of my thinking has been negative and around 'Why did I bother doing a PhD in the first place?' I am not quite sure that Nietzsche was right about adversity making you stronger, and I am sure you will find enough adversity in your life without taking on a PhD! I have been thinking that I should have perhaps focussed my time and effort on other goals. I have ambivalent feelings about the PhD and why I did it anyway—

perhaps for some negative reasons such as a lack of confidence in my own ability and needing to prove something to myself.

> *"What doesn't kill you makes you stronger."*
> - Friedrich Nietzsche, German philosopher

In writing this section, however, I get to reflect on the benefits I have gained from doing my PhD, which is a very useful exercise. I think many of the benefits from doing a PhD are common to setting and achieving any difficult goal. Any difficult goal forces you to change yourself if you want to achieve the goal. You need to confront your own weaknesses. For me the PhD was just like a personal mountain to climb. On the way to completing my goal were struggles and challenges, which I overcame. I learned to persist and keep going when things looked hopeless. *I think it's not that you get a PhD that matters; it's who you become as a result of getting the PhD that really counts.* In my opinion, the journey is much more important than the destination. Maybe I was looking for the benefits of my PhD in the wrong place. It's not the destination but the journey which is important. It's who you become as a result of doing the PhD.

I recently watched a talk by Diana Nyad. In 2013, on her fifth attempt and at age 64, she became the first person confirmed to swim from Cuba to Florida without the aid of a shark cage, swimming from Havana to Key West (110 miles or 180 km). To achieve that goal she had to become a different person. The achievement of such a difficult goal is a reflection of her inner world and strength of character. As I write this, I am reading a book written by Gerry Duffy, an Irishman who competed in a

DECA Iron Distance Triathlon—10 Ironman Challenges in 10 days. Each day for 10 consecutive days, competitors had to swim 3.8 km, cycle 190 km and run a full marathon of 42.2 km. Twenty started but only three finished. Gerry finished first by over 22 hours. According to Gerry, anyone stretching themselves to reach any difficult goal will be tested and grow from the experience of setting and achieving a difficult goal.

As I see it the same applies to doing a PhD—this is a difficult goal and will certainly test and stretch you and is an opportunity for personal growth. I now see a PhD not just as the mastery of a discipline, but also training of the mind. You must work independently and develop techniques of self-governance, as I have outlined in this book. Doing a PhD you design and manage your own project over a period of several years. On reflection, I am pleased with the skills and attitudes I have learned along the way which have propelled me to complete my PhD. However, the costs of these PhD benefits may be high and perhaps could be achieved in other ways which are faster and the payoff is better—starting and managing your own business, for example.

In any case, below are the ways which I have benefited from doing my PhD, including important skills and attitudes I have learned.

One's destination is never a place but rather a new way of looking at things.

- Henry Miller, American writer

I have earned an impressive credential

Having a PhD puts you into a small group of people relative to the whole population. For example, there were 176,945 people (of all ages) in Canada with earned doctorates at the time of the 2006 census. This represents something less than 1% of the adult population of the country (and is similar to the percentage of PhD holders in the USA as mentioned in Chapter One) —a very small segment of that population with PhDs (SSHRCC, 2013). I remember not too long ago being impressed—and I suppose also a small bit intimidated—by people who had PhDs. However, now that I have a PhD, when it comes to credentials, nobody is going to intimidate me. I no longer suffer from certification intimidation! I suppose to some extent I have also increased my personal status—it is an impressive achievement to complete a PhD and produce an original piece of research.

Now that I have completed my PhD and there is no more pain attached to it, I am hoping that someday it will impress someone or open a door to an opportunity for me that I would not have been otherwise able to get. The pain of the PhD was temporary but the reward is permanent—who knows how the doctorate will help me for the rest of my life.

Unless you try to do something beyond what you have already mastered, you will never grow.

- Ralph Waldo Emerson

I have developed my Grit

Grit is passion and perseverance for very long-term goals. Grit is having stamina, sticking with your future day in and day out for years despite failure and setbacks and working really hard. Grit is living life as if it's a marathon and not a sprint. One of the benefits of completing a PhD project is to be able to write a book like this one without batting an eyelid! After all, I have just come from six years of PhD study and written a 300+ page thesis, so the idea of writing this book was certainly less daunting. Skills I learned writing my PhD allowed me to write this book. I also know that I can tackle a big project and be confident that I can persist over a number of years to completion. When doing a PhD you learn to develop a tolerance for frustration that is necessary to your becoming a successful scientist. In science—but not only in science—we often learn the most from failure.

Success is the ability to go from one failure to another with no loss of enthusiasm.

- Sir Winston Churchill, British politician (1874-1965)

I have set and achieved a big goal

What I really learned was that your limits are in very large part determined by the size of the goals you set. Each time you accomplish a bigger goal, you realise that you can accomplish an even bigger goal. Unexpectedly, "I could never do that" becomes "I could someday do that" and ultimately "I will do that." That is the power of truly big goals. Completing difficult projects like a PhD gives confidence in your ability to complete other challenging goals. When it comes to setting goals, I'm not suggesting that everyone should do a PhD. It is time consuming and expensive and requires many trade-offs in other areas of your life. However, doing a PhD forces you to adopt new behaviours in order to succeed. The process has challenged me to expand my comfort zone and become someone better. I have found that the challenge of doing a PhD has resulted in my becoming more disciplined, more focused and more willing to set bigger goals. I have also learned how to manage my time better—doing a PhD makes you focus on your time because you need to get things done within agreed deadlines in order to make progress. Doing a PhD also helped me to be more focussed in the present moment, which is the only moment we can make progress. The PhD has also taught me how to visualise my goals and programme my subconscious mind for success. The biggest lesson is that if you set goals within your limits, you will only achieve goals within your limits. If you set goals that are far outside your perceived limits, you are surprisingly likely to achieve them.

Being more self-reflective

Overall, I believe that I am much more self-reflective as a result of doing my PhD. I do try to apply action research on myself. What I mean is that I carry out research on my own performance. At the end of each day I ask myself three questions. What did I plan to do today? What actually happened? What have I learned that I can apply to improving tomorrow? Doing a PhD as a challenging goal forces you to look at yourself. You are the key player in the PhD and if you are not making progress you need to change yourself before you can begin to move ahead. The new positive habits which I have developed as a result of doing the PhD are relevant to my achieving other goals in life as well. I am now applying habits and self-knowledge to achieve other life goals, and I certainly have a new confidence in myself that I can persist and achieve other tough goals.

Better at critical thinking

My mother made me a scientist without ever intending to. Every other Jewish mother in Brooklyn would ask her child after school: "So? Did you learn anything today?" But not my mother. "Izzy," she would say, "did you ask a good question today?" That difference —asking good questions—made me become a scientist.

- Isidor Isaac Rabi, Physicist

One of the more noticeable benefits of my doing a PhD is how I think about things. I am much more analytical in my thinking. The PhD process teaches you to adopt a state of mind that allows you to think logically, objectively and factually and to question things more. This comes from my ideas being questioned and challenged by my supervisors and examiners during my PhD and when writing my peer reviewed paper. At the early stages of my PhD I feared—and attempted to avoid— being questioned and probed. However, due to the PhD I now absolutely welcome my ideas and writings being questioned and challenged. I realise this is the way to improvement, and if someone points out a weakness they are doing you a favour!

When I hear people make sweeping statements I always question the evidence behind what they are saying. What I have noticed is that people often make statements without much thought and when you question how they know something they are stumped.

I am also now a much more critical judge of the writing of others. When writers make statements unsupported by sufficient evidence it really stands out for me. Since completing the PhD I have peer reviewed a number of research papers. The ability to critically analyse the writing of others is a very useful skill that I have gained as a result of doing my PhD. The PhD process has taught me to question things more, and indeed, the confidence to be able to question the value of the PhD itself!

I have learned valuable skills and specialist knowledge

Of course, when you do a PhD you are also learning a variety of research and related skills. The ability to use sophisticated methodologies toward the delivery of a thesis has wide-ranging uses. Doing a PhD is very hands on. You are under the tutelage of an experienced researcher who gives you one-to-one constructive feedback on your work. You get to think things through as there is sufficient time to delve deeply into your subject area and learn research methods. You get to make mistakes and reflect on them and how you could do things better the next time. You learn how to plan out your research well, including budgeting and how to make a successful grant application. You learn skills in hypothesis formulation and experimental design. You learn how to analyse your data and use research software. You also learn valuable scientific writing skills. Scientific writing is a skill that requires a lot of practice and the endurance to face failure and respond positively. One of the writing skills I have learned in particular is how to write succinctly. This is a discipline you learn when you have to write a research paper with strict word limits.

Along the way to PhD completion, students also present sections of their work at seminars and conferences and often in lectures to undergraduate audiences. In each case the level of the presentation must be altered to suit the audience and purpose. PhD students also develop important skills in teaching and mentoring undergraduate students.

Overall, the PhD develops skills in original and critical thinking, effective communication, creativity, empathy, innovation, problem solving, project management, and leadership (McGill University, 2013).

All the above skills gained from doing a PhD also enhance your ability to 'learn how to learn,' which is a very important skill to secure and retain employment in a fast changing world. There are fewer full time jobs, and workers need to be more flexible and adaptable.

'Learning how to learn is life's most important skill.'

- Tony Buzan

Apart from the skills I have learned, I have also developed specialist knowledge on my subject area—African beekeeping development. Because of doing my PhD I have focussed on this particular subject area for six years as part of my study. I have read every article, book, research study I could find on this and related subjects numerous times. I have talked to specialists in my subject area. I have carried out my own original research and published this research. All of this focussed effort deepens your knowledge and expertise on your subject area and is a valuable legacy of doing a PhD, provided you are in a position to use your expertise/there is a demand for expertise in your subject area (choose wisely!).

Satisfaction at making a contribution

I am proud of the small contribution to knowledge that I made on African beekeeping, which was the subject area of my PhD research. I wrote a book aimed to support ordinary small scale beekeepers in Kenya and other African countries in improving their livelihoods through beekeeping. I developed a website (www.apiconsult.com) to support African beekeepers with up-to-date information. I carried out primary research relevant to small scale African beekeepers, wrote my PhD thesis and published a peer reviewed research paper. I feel that I made a useful contribution to knowledge on African beekeeping and livelihoods that others can learn from and build upon. There is a satisfaction on focussing your time and energy on one subject area and making a small contribution to knowledge in that area. Doing a PhD gave me the opportunity to deepen my knowledge and make that contribution, and I am grateful for that opportunity.

The downside of doing a PhD

It can seem great to have a PhD and get to call yourself 'Doctor.' However, getting a PhD has a number of significant downsides, as explored throughout this book. The key downsides to getting a PhD are summarised in this section.

There is a high opportunity cost to getting a PhD

A major downside to doing a PhD is the high opportunity cost. The opportunity cost is the loss of other alternatives when one alternative is chosen (the opportunity cost of doing a PhD has been explored at length in Chapter Two). When you embark on a PhD you are going to spend years on this project and invest significant amounts of money and time over a period of years— six years in my case. This is a significant cost and perhaps you may be better off investing the same money, time and effort into some other project (s). The rewards in terms of enhanced career prospects for investing in a PhD may not warrant the investment of money, time and sheer effort required. Students should consider whether a doctoral program is really suited to their personal goals, interests and labour market aspirations. Therefore, do your career planning before embarking on your PhD and be clear of the reality of the likely career prospects post your PhD. To help you make this decision seek out current students and recent graduates for information on their experiences. Ask for available statistics on labour market outcomes and career pathways of recently graduated students for your particular programme of interest. Compare the likely benefits of investing in a PhD with the likely benefits of investing the same money time and effort in alternative projects.

Will anyone care about my research?

I am proud of my contribution to expanding knowledge through my PhD research. However, how my contribution gets put into practice is another issue. I struggled for years researching my topic, and I published part of my PhD research in a peer reviewed journal over a year ago now as I write this. In that time I have received no queries on the research paper as corresponding author. It leaves me wondering if the people who need to read my research have actually read it. I suspect in the meantime a lot of money has been wasted on poorly designed beekeeping projects which could have benefited from a close look at my research findings. I have made my contribution, but will those who should read it actually bother to read my paper?

Next steps

You are invited to visit my website, www.lifeisalaboratory.com for further updates and information on life after doing a PhD. On this website I will continue to post updates on my life after the PhD and reflections at different milestones post the completion of my PhD. I am conscious that my perceptions of doing the PhD may change over time as, for example, the memory of the pain of doing the PhD may fade and I perhaps focus more on the benefits. I also invite you to check out the useful resources listed at the back of this book. There are many sources of further information on the PhD process—books, articles and websites. There are also resources on wider issues such as planning, goal setting, achievement, personal development and success in general.

Finally, I would like to thank you for taking the time to read this book and hope that my experiences and reflections shared in these pages have given you a better understanding of the PhD process. I wish you the very best in your life's journey whether or not you are embarking on a PhD, continuing with your PhD or 'letting go' of your PhD. This is your one and only life and as the saying goes 'life is not a dress rehearsal,' so you must make the best decision for you.

About the Author

Tom Carroll grew up on a farm in rural County Laois in the midlands of Ireland. He attended university in Dublin where he studied for a bachelor's degree in Agricultural Science. He later completed a master's degree in Environmental Resource Management. In 1993 he moved to Kenya as a volunteer, working on rural development/poverty alleviation programmes, with a particular focus on beekeeping as a means to diversify the livelihoods of poor households. From 2001 to 2003 he completed a master's degree in Entrepreneurial Studies by Distance Learning from Stirling University, Scotland. Spurred on by successfully completing this latter degree he decided to register for a PhD, which he began in 2006 while working in Kenya and supporting a wife and three young children. In 2008 the whole family moved from Kenya back to Ireland, changing home, schools, jobs and careers in the process. Despite the challenges of this transition, Tom successfully completed his PhD studies in 2012.

Contact the Author/Leave Feedback

You are welcome to contact the author of this book/leave feedback on the book at the following website: www.lifeisalaboratory.com/monkey

References and Useful Resources

While I was working on my own PhD and also while writing this book, I encountered many useful resources such as books, reports and websites related to the issues concerning PhD study, many of them referenced throughout this book. I have listed these references and useful resources in this section to provide further support/reading material on the topics covered in this book. I have also listed here useful resources which do not specifically deal with the PhD but which are relevant and important to success with any major goal in life, such as time management and personal effectiveness. You might want to dip in and out of these articles on an as-needed basis. Links to online resources are correct at the time of writing although resources may be moved or removed later. In such cases if you Google the article title, chances are good that you will find them at their new location.

Useful PhD related Books and Articles

Listed below are useful PhD related articles, books and reports.

- Almeida-Souza, Leonardo and Baets, Jonathan (2012), PhD survival guide: Some brief advice for PhD students. EMBO reports, Volume 13, Issue 3, pages 189–192, European Molecular Biology Organisation. Available online at: http://onlinelibrary.wiley.com/doi/10.1038/embor.2012.15/abstract

- ASSA (2010), The PhD Study: An evidence-based study on how to meet the demands for high-level skills in an emerging economy, The Academy of Science for South Africa.
- Auriol, Laudeline (2010), Careers of Doctorate Holders: Employment and Mobility Patterns STI Working Paper 2010/4. Organisation for Economic Co-operation and Development. Available online at: www.oecd.org/sti/working-papers
- Azuma, Ronald T. (2003), A graduate school survival guide: 'So long, and thanks for the Ph.D!' Available online at: http://www.cs.unc.edu/~azuma/hitch4.html
- Bair, C. R., & Haworth, J. G. (November, 1999). Doctoral student attrition and persistence: A metasynthesis of research. Paper presented at the annual meeting of the Association for the Study of Higher Education. San Antonio, TX.
- Basalla, Susan and Maggie Debelius (2007), *So What Are You Going to Do with That?: Finding Careers Outside Academia*. Chicago: University of Chicago Press.
- Bolker, Joan (1998), *Writing Your Dissertation in Fifteen Minutes a Day: A Guide to Starting, Revising, and Finishing Your Doctoral Thesis*, Owl Books, New York.
- Brabazon, Tara (2013), '10 truths a PhD supervisor will never tell you.' The Times Higher Education. Available online at: http://www.timeshighereducation.co.uk/features/10-truths-a-phd-supervisor-will-never-tell-you/2005513.article

- Casey, Bernard H. (2009), 'The economic contribution of PhDs,' Journal of Higher Education Policy and Management, 31:3,219 – 227.

- Clance, Rose and Imes, Suzanne (1978), 'The Imposter Phenomenon in High Achieving Women: Dynamics and Therapeutic Intervention' Psychotherapy Theory, Research and Practice. Volume 15, #3, Fall 1978.

- Deloitte (2010), 'The Researchers Report 2012 – Scorecards.' DG Research and Innovation Monitor human resources policies and practices in research (LOT 1 Part 1). Available online at: http://ec.europa.eu/euraxess/pdf/research_policies/121 003_Scorecards_ALL_FINAL.pdf

- Department of Education and Skills (2011), National Strategy for Higher Education to 2030, Report of the Strategy Group, Dublin.

- Dimsdale, J. E., & Young, M. D. (2006). Student Mental Health Committee Final Report. University of California. Available online at: http://regents.universityofcalifornia.edu/regmeet/sept0 6/303attach.pdf

- Dolin, Eric Jay (2011), *The Ph.D. Survival Guide*, Amazon Digital Services, Inc.

- Foley, Greg (2013), *The Education Conundrum - One academic's thoughts on a wicked problem*, Amazon Edition.

- Forfas (2009), The Role of PhDs in the Smart Economy. Advisory Council for Science, Technology and

Innovation, Forfas, Dublin. Available online at: http://www.forfas.ie/media/asco91215_role_of_phds.pdf

- Gallagher, Mary (2012), *Academic, Armageddon: An Irish Requiem for Higher Education*. The Liffey Press, Dublin, 250pp.

- Gannon, Frank (2006), What is a PhD? EMBO reports, 7 (11), European Molecular Biology Organization Available online at: http://onlinelibrary.wiley.com/doi/10.1038/sj.embor.74 00842/pdf

- Gill, P., & Burnard, P. (2008). The student-supervisor relationship in the PhD/Doctoral process. British Journal of Nursing, 17(10).

- Golde, C. M. (2000). Should I stay or should I go? Student descriptions of the doctoral attrition process. The Review of Higher Education, 23(2), 199-227.

- Higher Education Authority (2013 A), Towards a Performance Evaluation Framework: Profiling Irish Higher Education, Dublin.

- Higher Education Authority (2013 B), What Do Graduates Do? The Class of 2012. An Analysis of the Universities First Destination of Graduates Survey 2013, Dublin. Available online at: http://www.hea.ie/sites/default/files/what_do_graduates_do_2012.pdf

- Irish Universities Association (IUA) (2004), The Future of the PhD in Ireland—attracting and retaining post-graduate researchers in Irish Universities. Proceedings of a Conference Held by Conference of Heads of Irish Universities (C.H.I.U.).

- Kadison, R., & Foy DiGeronimo, T. (2004). *College of the Overwhelmed: The Campus Mental Health Crisis and What to Do About It*. San Francisco: Jossey-Bass.

- Lovitts, B. (2001). *Leaving the Ivory Tower: The Causes and Consequences of Departure from Doctoral Study*. Lanham, MD: Rowman & Littlefield Publishers, Inc.

- Lovallo, D., Kahneman, D (2003). 'Delusions of Success: How Optimism Undermines Executives' Decisions.' Harvard Business Review: 56–63.

- Maldonado, V., Wiggers, R., & Arnold, C. (2013). 'So You Want to Earn a PhD? The Attraction, Realities, and Outcomes of Pursuing a Doctorate.' Toronto: Higher Education Quality Council of Ontario.

- Mason, Mary Ann (2012), 'The Future of the Ph.D., The Chronicle of Higher Education.' Available online at: http://chronicle.com/article/The-Future-of-the-PhD/131749/

- McGill University (2013), White Paper on the Future of the PhD in the Humanities. Institute for the Public Life of Arts and Ideas. December 2013.

- Miller, Alison B. (2013), 'Finish Your Dissertation Once and for All!: How to Overcome Psychological Barriers, Get Results, and Move on With Your Life,' American Psychological Association.

- Myers, L. H. (1999). Barriers to completion of the doctoral degree in educational administration. Dissertation. Retrieved from:

http://scholar.lib.vt.edu/theses/available/etd-041699-125349/unrestricted/LHMyers.PDF

- Noble, K. A. (1994). *Changing doctoral degrees: An international perspective.* Buckingham: SRHE & Open University Press.

- Cyranoski D, Gilbert N, Ledford H, Nayar A, Yahia M. (2011), 'The PhD factory,' Nature, Apr 21; 472 (7343): 276-9. doi: 10.1038/472276a.

- O'shaughnessy, Lynn (2012), '12 reasons not to get a PhD,' Moneywatch, CBS News. Available online at: http://www.cbsnews.com/8301-505145_162-57468913/12-reasons-not-to-get-a-phd/

- Peironcely, Julio (2012), Graduate School Advice Series: '10 Things You Should Know Before Starting A PhD.' Available online at:
 http://www.nextscientist.com/graduate-school-advice-series-starting-phd/

- Peters, Robert (1997), *Getting What You Came For: The Smart Student's Guide to Earning an M.A. or a Ph.D.* Revised edition, Farrar, Straus and Giroux, New York.

- Pfeffer, Jeffrey and Christina T. Fong (2002), 'The End of Business Schools? Less Success Than Meets the Eye,' ACAD MANAG LEARN EDU September 1, 2002 1:1 78-95;
 http://www.aomonline.org/Publications/Articles/BSchools.asp

- Shepherd, Jessica (2007), 'A Race to the Finish,' The Guardian, Tuesday 2 October 2007. Available online at:

http://www.theguardian.com/education/2007/oct/02/highereducation.postgraduate

- SSHRCC (2013) White Paper on the Future of the PhD in the Humanities. Social Sciences and Humanities Research Council of Canada.
- Sokol, Daniel K. (2012), 'Is a PhD the Right Option for You?' The Guardian Newspaper. Available online at: http://careers.guardian.co.uk/phd-right-career-option
- Stock, Wendy A., T. Aldrich Finegan, and John J. Siegfried (2009), 'Completing an Economics PhD in Five Years: let the Data (literally) speak for themselves.' American Economic Review: Papers & Proceedings 2009, 99:2, 624–629.
- Tamburri, Rosanna (2013), 'The PhD is in need of revision.' University Affairs. Available from: http://www.universityaffairs.ca/the-phd-is-in-need-of-revision.aspx#latest_data
- Taylor, Mark C. (2011), 'Reform the PhD system or close it down,' Nature 472, 261 (2011) Published online 20 April 2011 doi:10.1038/472261a.
- The Economist (2010), 'The disposable academic - Why doing a PhD is often a waste of time' The Economist Magazine, December 16th 2010 Edition. Available online at: http://www.economist.com/node/17723223?story_id=17723223
- UCD Graduate Studies (No date) 'Doctoral Studies in UCD - The Structured PhD.' University College Dublin. Available online at:

http://www.ucd.ie/t4cms/UCD%20Graduate%20Studies%20Structured%20PhD%20leaflet%202011.pdf

- Van der Boom, H., G. Klabbers, K. Putnik, M. Woolderink, (2013), 'It takes two to tango - A qualitative study amongst PhD candidates and supervisors to evaluate the process of PhD supervision in the Netherlands,' Maastricht University. Available online at: http://www.maastrichtuniversity.nl/web/show/id=6998551/langid=42.

- Willis, Brad and Carmichael, Karla D. (2011), 'The Lived Experience of Late-Stage Doctoral Student Attrition in Counselor Education.' The Qualitative Report, Volume 16 Number 1 January 2011 192-207.

PhD/Education Related Online Resources

Listed below are useful online resources such as websites and blogs related to doing a PhD.

- **FindAPhD** is a platform for universities from anywhere in the world to promote and advertise their English-taught research projects and international PhD programmes. The site is based in the UK and is useful for those searching for a PhD programme. See their website: http://www.findaphd.com/student/study/study-16.asp

- **Matt Might** is Assistant Professor at the University of Utah in the United States. His subject area is "static analysis of higher-order programs." Don't ask me to explain that but it has applications in Internet security. His blog has many useful general articles including the one linked to below: '3 qualities of successful Ph.D. students: Perseverance, tenacity and cogency.' http://matt.might.net/articles/successful-phd-students/

- **The Professor Is In** is the website of Karen L. Kelsky, Ph.D. Karen is a former university professor in the USA. Her website contains a variety of useful articles related to doing a PhD. Karen provides a range of academic services such as academic editing. Karen also provides one-on-one advice for PhD students. http://theprofessorisin.com/

- **The Thesis Whisperer** described as a 'blog newspaper dedicated to the topic of doing a thesis.' The blog is edited by Dr. Inger Mewburn, Director of research training at the Australian National University. There are many articles and resources of value on doing a PhD. http://thesiswhisperer.com/.

    One particular article I found useful was: 'What to say when someone asks you: "Should I do a PhD?"' http://thesiswhisperer.com/2011/11/07/should-i-do-a-phd/

- **TRANS-DOC project,** funded by Erasmus Mundus programme of the European Union. The site has a number of documents and PowerPoint presentations on trans-Atlantic cooperation in doctoral training. http://www.coimbra-group.eu/transdoc/

- **The PhD Movie** - *Piled Higher and Deeper* (PhD) is an American comic movie following the lives of a number of PhD students and their professor. It costs $5 USD to watch. Laugh with caution—that might be you and your PhD supervisor now or in the future! http://www.phdmovie.com/

There is also a PhD related comic strip—see: http://phdcomics.com/comics.php

- This is the blog of **Tanya Maria Golash-Boza**, Associate Professor of Sociology, University of California. Maria has an impressive list of publications which she is working on and which have already been published. Her daily writing plan is a useful guide for any PhD student. She is also a mother and manages to balance her different roles. Please see: http://getalifephd.blogspot.ie/

- This is a useful blog posting by **Nathan Yau** called 'A Survival Guide to Starting and Finishing a PhD.' The blog posting is available online at: http://flowingdata.com/2013/04/01/a-survival-guide-to-starting-and-finishing-a-phd/

- **100 Reasons NOT to Go to Graduate School.** This blog is an attempt to offer those considering graduate school some good reasons to do something else. Its focus is on the humanities and social sciences. If you need more reasons not to do a PhD—read this blog! Please see: http://100rsns.blogspot.ie/

- **Life After the PhD** is a blog dedicated to providing career advice for graduate students who are considering leaving the academy. It features interviews with PhDs who have gone onto successful careers outside of academia, as well as other career resources. Please see: http://lifeafterthephd.com/

- **The Versatile PhD.** This is a web-based, woman-owned, socially positive business that helps universities provide graduate students with non-academic professional development. Their mission is to help graduate students and new PhDs identify, prepare for, and excel in possible non-academic careers. Please see: http://versatilephd.com/

Other Useful Books and Articles

Listed below are books and articles I have found useful related to personal development which are not specifically related to doing a PhD. However, the ideas and skills advocated in these articles are nonetheless important for PhD success, or indeed, success in completing any project.

- Arden, John B. (2010), *Rewire Your Brain: Think Your Way to a Better Life*. Wiley.

- Banfield, Edward C (1970), *The Unheavenly City: The Nature and the Future of Our Urban Crisis*. Little Brown & Co.

- Bolles, Richard Nelson (2014), *What Color Is Your Parachute? A Practical Manual for Job-Hunters and Career-Changers*. Ten Speed Press.

- Bornstein, Brian H. and Chapman, Gretchin B., (1995), 'Learning Lessons From Sunk Costs.' Faculty Publications, Department of Psychology. Paper 294. http://digitalcommons.unl.edu/psychfacpub/294

- Brown , Brene (2012), *Daring Greatly: How the Courage to Be Vulnerable Transforms the Way We Live, Love, Parent, and Lead*. Gotham.

- Collins, Jim and Jerry I. Porras (2004), *Built to Last: Successful Habits of Visionary Companies*. Harper Business.

- Covey Stephen R., (1990), *The 7 Habits of Highly Effective People, Powerful Lessons in Personal Change*, Simon & Schuster, New York.

- Duffy, Gerry (2011), *Who Dares, Runs: The Remarkable Story of a Man Who Went from 50 Lbs Overweight to Running 32 Marathons in 32 Consecutive Days*, Ballpoint Press.

- Duhigg, Charles (2012), *The Power of Habit: Why We Do What We Do in Life and Business*. Random House.

- Dweck, Carol (2006), Mindset: *The New Psychology Of Success—How We Can Learn To Fulfill Our Potential*, Random House Books.

- Ericsson, K. Anders; Krampe, Ralf T.; Tesch-Römer, Clemens (1993), 'The role of deliberate practice in the acquisition of expert performance.' Psychological Review, Vol 100(3), 363-406.

- Flannery, Pierce (2008), *Grabbing the Oyster! Anecdotes and Advice from Icons of Irish Business*. Oak Tree Press.

- Ford, Martin (2009), *The Lights in the Tunnel: Automation, Accelerating Technology and the Economy of the Future*, CreateSpace Independent Publishing Platform.

- Grunburg, Martin (2010), *The Habit Factor: An Innovative Method to Align Habits with Goals to Achieve Success*. Equilibrium Enterprises.

- Hill, Napoleon (1937), *Think and Grow Rich*, Napoleon Hill Foundation.

- Kaufman, Josh (2012), *The Personal MBA: Master the Art of Business*. Penguin Group (USA). Note: The book focusses on learning business skills without doing the MBA and getting into debt—very useful website and resources related to business. http://personalmba.com/

- Olson, Jeff (2011), *The Slight Edge (Revised Edition): Turning Simple Disciplines Into Massive Success*. Success Books.

- Ries, Eric (2011), *The Lean Startup*. Penguin UK.

- Schwartz, David Joseph (1987), *The Magic of Thinking Big*. Fireside; Reprint edition.

- Tracy, Brian (2007), *Eat That Frog! 21 Great Ways to Stop Procrastinating and Get More Done in Less Time*. Berrett-Koehler Publishers.

Useful Online Resources

The following online resources on a variety of personal development/personal effectiveness topics were found to be useful.

1. Angel Lee Duckworth - Grit

Angela Lee Duckworth is a Psychologist at the University of Pennsylvania who studies intangible concepts such as self-control and grit to determine how they might predict both

academic and professional success. Grit is a key factor in any endeavour, including getting a PhD.
http://www.ted.com/talks/angela_lee_duckworth_the_key_to_success_grit

2. Brené Brown - Vulnerability

There are two very good talks here by Brené Brown, a professor at the University of Houston Graduate College of Social Work. Why your critics aren't the ones who count and how to be vulnerable. I had to learn to be vulnerable by sharing my work with my PhD supervisor. Without doing this I could not make progress. When you publish your work you are also vulnerable to criticism. To achieve anything you have to learn to be vulnerable.
http://99u.com/videos/20052/brene-brown-stop-focusing-on-your-critics

http://www.ted.com/talks/brene_brown_on_vulnerability.html

3. Gurdy.net - Mindfulness

This website is run by an Irishman called Willie Horton. Willie is an expert on mindfulness. The only time we have is the present moment. You can only work on your PhD in the present moment so learn how to be present! I start each day with one of Willie's mental exercises. See: www.gurdy.net

4. Learning to Love Rejection

Brian Martin is professor of social sciences at the University of Wollongong, in Australia. In this article Brian discussed the need for academics to be more open about rejection. When people hide rejection many scholars, especially the less experienced ones, have naive expectations.

Read more:
http://www.insidehighered.com/advice/2013/07/08/essay-importance-rejection-academic-careers#ixzz2x2u3gt8M

5. The Habit Factor

This is the website of Martin Grunburg, Entrepreneur, author, speaker and coach. Our habits define us and your PhD related habits will carry you to success or failure. Martin also has a useful habit app for your smartphone, which allows you to set and track habits. www.thehabitfactor.com

6. Visualisation/hypnotherapy

In this book I mentioned having trained as a hypnotherapist while doing my PhD (doing other unrelated courses alongside your PhD is not a good idea!). You can use hypnotherapy to programme your subconscious mind in a variety of ways. For example, you can visualise completion of your PhD goal or if you have to give a presentation and are feeling nervous, you could use hypnotherapy to overcome your fears. The link below is to a site where you can buy pre-recorded self-hypnosis scripts on a variety of topics. http://www.uncommon-knowledge.co.uk/

Useful computer software

There are many computer software packages /smartphone apps which you will find useful while working on your PhD. Some of these are obvious, such as word processing, statistical analysis and spreadsheet software packages. Listed here are some additional software packages/smartphone apps which I found useful in helping me to achieve my PhD goal.

1. GoalEnforcer

Goal Enforcer is a visual goal-setting software. I found this software very easy and intuitive to use. I did much of my PhD planning and brainstorming in GoalEnforcer. You can try out the software for free. http://www.goalenforcer.com/

2. Mendeley

Mendeley is a reference manager and academic social network that can help you organise your research, collaborate with others online, and discover the latest research. This is the software I used to organise my academic references for my PhD. I found it very useful and best of all for the hard pressed student, it's free! http://www.mendeley.com/

3. Mind movies

This website offers you a quick and easy way to create a short video to help you visualise achieving your PhD goal. According to their website a mind movie is a 'Digital Video Vision Board Filled with Positive Affirmations, Inspiring Images and Motivating Music.' See 'Reinforcing your PhD vision' in Chapter Four of this book for further discussion on mind movies. www.mindmovies.com

4. Pomodoro Technique

This is the technique of chunking down your work into manageable pieces using a smartphone app. The following is a link to one particular app which I used, called 'Pomodoroido,'

available on Google Play (there are many others which you can try out as well).
https://play.google.com/store/apps/details?id=net.artifix.pomodroido.free

You can also read further and buy a physical Pomodoro timer – see: http://pomodorotechnique.com/

See Chapter Four of this book, 'Chunk down your work,' for a discussion on how I used the Pomodoro technique to help me progress my PhD.

5. XMind

XMind is a very good mind mapping software. You can use the software to map out all your PhD related ideas and attach relevant documents to your mind map. The free version of this software is very functional. I used this tool for mapping out concepts related to my PhD and organising all the relevant material related to a particular concept. http://www.xmind.net/

Made in the USA
Monee, IL
29 October 2023